RESCRIPT

Daily Goal Getting & Productivity Planner

Dr. Colleen Georges

Copyright © 2023 Colleen Georges, Ed.D.
All rights reserved.

Printed in the United States of America
Published by RESCRIPT Your Story LLC
Piscataway, NJ 08854

Cover design by Debbie O'Byrne at https://JetLaunch.net

Visit the author's website at www.ColleenGeorges.com

All rights reserved. No part of this publication may be reproduced, stored in a retrieval system, or transmitted in any form or by any means—for example, electronic, photocopy, recording—without the prior written permission of the publisher. The only exception is brief quotations in printed reviews.

Paperback ISBN-13: 978-1-7375281-9-7

RESCRIPT

Daily Goal Getting & Productivity Planner

Dr. Colleen Georges

Using the RESCRIPT Daily Goal Getting & Productivity Planner

The RESCRIPT Daily Goal Getting & Productivity Planner is all about engaging your goals. The planner allows you to decide what you want to accomplish in each area of your life, offers goal-getting strategies, and gives you tools to create productivity habits that get things done!

The planner includes **365+ days** for you to set and get your goals and track your productivity. It can be used on its own or as a companion to my 2019 award-winning book, *RESCRIPT the Story You're Telling Yourself*, which includes an in-depth chapter on Engaging Your Goals. **Every week begins with motivational quotes from inspiring people and brief revelations from goal setting research studies.**

The planner has a 3 Ps Weekly Action Agenda for each week of the year and a Commitment Calendar for each day of the year. Every Sunday, you can sit down somewhere quiet and create your 3 Ps Weekly Action Agenda for that week, writing in the date, and then writing in your "have to do" and "want to do" goals for the week.

- **Professional:** Actions related to work and/or school that are "have to dos".
- **Personal:** Actions related to home tasks, and personal, family, or friend related errands or phone calls to make that are "have to dos".
- **Passions:** Actions related to your Passion Projects/Goals in any area of life - your "want to do" goals!

Designate a day of the week you will have the action completed by. Establishing a date of completion is critically important—this is going to help you prioritize what needs to get done first and what actions can wait a bit longer. Make sure your actions are broken down into smaller steps that feel less overwhelming! If there are additional action items that pop up during the week—the unexpected undertakings—you can add them to your list as the week goes along and assign them completion dates as well.

Your list should only focus on this week, as not to overwhelm you with items that are not yet priorities. So, for projects or tasks that are longer term (two weeks away or more) that you want a running visual reminder so you don't forget, use the Longer Term Projects or Actions section at the bottom of your Action Agenda. These longer term items do not need to be chunked down into smaller tasks yet, you can keep them broad for now (until they become higher priority).

After completing your Action Agenda, take a look at your Commitment Calendar for each day of the week to determine where you will dedicate time to your Weekly Action Agenda items. Plot it out. I suggest using pencil so you can make any needed modifications throughout the week. Each morning, you can revisit your daily Commitment Calendar, make any needed edits, and write down your top three goals for the day, words you're empowering yourself with, ways you're motivating yourself, and ways you're bringing joy into your life that day.

As you complete a task, cross it off on your Weekly Action Agenda! This action feels good—it lets you feel successful and motivates you to keep going, knowing YOU CAN DO THIS! And, at the end of the week when you see all those crossed off lines, you'll see how much you accomplished in just one week. In your Commitment Calendar at the end of the week, you can write down your proudest accomplishments, obstacles and challenges you triumphed over, ways you were kind to yourself and others, and what you're most grateful for that week!

Goal Getting Strategies

Pledge to Pass Up Permission

Only YOU know what you really want, need, & are capable of. You run you—no one else runs you. If you want it, that's enough. Now go get it!

"Will" it into the World

When you hear yourself say you're *thinking about, planning to, gonna try* to work on your goal, amplify your Inner Advocate, & restate passionately – "I WILL!"

Salvage Success Strategies

How have you achieved goals before? How did you push past fears, create time, & move through challenges? The answers to reaching your new goals may exist in strategies you've used before.

Triumph Tracker

How often do you write down your accomplishments? We're fueled by our successes & triumphs. In acknowledging, tracking, & savoring them, we boost our confidence to tackle our next big goals!

Seek a Success Sidekick

Do you know anyone looking to reach a similar or even a different goal? Ask if they'd like to partner up! You could text one another at the start & end of each day to motivate one another & check on progress!

Daydream Your Desired Destinations

When we daydream our desired destinations, put them into words, & envision them in our minds, we can make more informed decisions aligned authentically with who we are & what we truly want.

Define Your Desired Destinations' Design

Set positive, precise, pragmatic goals. Positive—what you "do want" & "will do." Precise—exactly what, how, & when. Pragmatic— stretches skills & comfort zone, while remaining achievable.

Realization Roadmap

Develop "If/Then" or "When/Then" statements to define when, where, & how you'll achieve goal-related tasks. Connecting them with actions you already take as part of your regular routine helps.

3 Ps Weekly Action Agenda

Each Sunday, create your 3 Ps (Professional, Personal, Passions) Weekly Action Agenda by jotting down small steps to complete your larger goals. As you complete a task, CROSS IT OFF!

Commitment Calendar

Create a Commitment Calendar by plotting out your typical daily tasks (e.g., meetings, classes) & scheduling specific time slots to work on tasks from your 3 Ps Weekly Action Agenda. Build in some buffer time for the unexpected.

Lead with the Least Labor

Work on tasks on your list that require the least amount of time & effort first. Then you can cross these off your list & feel a quicker sense of accomplishment!

Tackle the Toughest Task

Try tackling the toughest task first! Once you complete that more effortful task, you will feel an immense sense of accomplishment for getting it over & done with. Then all the other tasks will seem like nothing in comparison!

One Task at a Time

Your physical, mental, & emotional health will suffer if you try to do it all at once! Spread out your goal-related tasks to make them manageable, reasonable, achievable, & healthy.

Brief Brain Breaks

What is a brain break? It could be laying down or sitting back in your work chair with your eyes closed, sitting outside, or taking a quick nature walk. 15 minutes will do. During that time, keep your mind thinking peacefully & calmly & take a brain break from work tasks.

Compensate Completion

Brainstorm a list of big and little things you enjoy doing, or want to do, that can be used as compensations for completing the steps to your goal & the achievement of your goal. Use these rewards only after your completions.

Time Thief Tracker

We all have time thieves (e.g., social media, game apps). For one week, track how you spend your time, tally up time spent on time thieves, & then allocate time periods & limits for them.

Unexpected Undertakings Tracker

Track time spent on unexpected undertakings each week (e.g., car mechanic appt.), tally it up, & build enough buffer time into your schedule each day for the unexpected.

Rise & Round-Off the Day Routines

Create morning & evening routines. At day's end, tackle organizing & preparing tasks. Integrate connecting, relaxing, reflecting, & gratitude activities. In the morning, include exercise, planning, or inspiring activities. You decide what works for you!

Destination Designing Rituals

Select a location to travel to annually or quarterly, like a woodsy cabin or the beach, & take inventory & celebrate what you achieved toward your goals in the last few months or year & establish your goals for the next year or quarter.

Dream Depiction

Creating a Dream Depiction (vision board) is a fun way to represent your goals. Get some poster board, magazines, & art supplies. Cut & paste words & pictures related to goals. Use your Dream Depiction daily for inspiration!

Create Your Rise & Round-Off the Day Routines

Routines propel success. The ways we kick off and culminate our days have an important impact on what we accomplish. Those who are most productive generally begin and end their days with a particular self-customized routine. Starting your own custom Rise & Round-Off the Day Routine is a great way to reach your goals! Most morning or evening routines are approximately 30 minutes to a few hours in length, depending on what you would like to accomplish during those times. So, the first step is deciding what types of activities you want to incorporate into your routines. I am providing some possible activities below that could be incorporated into Rise and Round-Off Routines.

For Round-Off the Day Routines, tackling decision making tasks is a smart choice, such as selecting and laying out your outfit and/or kids' outfits for the following day, determining the next day's meal items, and making your lunch and/or kids' lunch for the following day. This ensures less rushing around in the morning. A different kind of decision-making task to include in your evening routine is planning out what you want to accomplish the following day—things related to your "have to do" tasks and your "want to do" goal-related actions. This helps you feel more prepared for the following day. Another thing you can include in an evening routine is tasks related to straightening up the house, like folding and putting away laundry, washing or putting away dishes, and putting away miscellaneous items that are laying around the house. If you spend 10 to 20 minutes on these tasks each evening, it stops things from piling up and feeling overwhelming. Maintaining order also means things are easier to find and feels less chaotic overall, as a mess in the home often contributes to frazzled thoughts in our brains.

Moreover, a great way to round off your day is to do something fun, such as reading a book you love, watching a show you enjoy, listening to a radio program you love, or engaging in a hobby. This is a little way to unwind and reward yourself for a day well spent. Doing something that relaxes you at the end of your night is nice as well, like drinking a cup of decaffeinated tea or sprinkling some relaxing essential oils on your pillow just before bed. Additionally, you might consider ending your day with some inspiration, such as watching a TED Talk, listening to an inspirational podcast episode, or reading some positive affirmations. This helps to keep your mind on things that are positive and motivational. Another thing that is calming and positive to do before bed is contemplate what you are grateful for that day. And, if you live with family, you will want to incorporate family time into your evening routine, as well as making sure your routine includes disconnecting from doing work for your job.

It's important to note that planning out your sleep time is also critical. Research suggests that somewhere between 6.5 and 8 hours of sleep is best for our health and productivity.

Let's say you go to sleep about 11pm. Here is a sample Round-Off the Day Routine:
- 8:00pm: Get the kids showered/bathed, in pajamas, & put the kids to bed.
- 8:45pm: Straighten up around the house.
- 9pm: Watch a sitcom with my partner while drinking a cup of decaf tea.
- 9:30pm: Plan out tomorrow's "have to do" & "want to do" goals in my Commitment Calendar.
- 9:45pm: Write in my Gratitude Journal.
- 10:00pm: Make tomorrow's lunches & select/lay out tomorrow's clothes.
- 10:30pm: Wash my face, brush my teeth, & put on pajamas.
- 10:45pm: Sprinkle pillow with Lavender essential oils & lay my head on my pillow to go to sleep.

Now, let's talk about some things you might consider for your daily Rise Routine. Much like your evening routine, your morning routine should include some inspirational activities like gratitude, affirmations, manifestos, and/or an inspiring video or audio book. Also like your evening routine, if you live with family, you will want to incorporate time talking and connecting with your family members. If you set your day's tasks and goals in advance the evening before, you can review them during your morning routine, and possibly spend some time working towards one of your goals/passion projects. This will get you feeling organized and give you an immediate sense of accomplishment as you begin your day!

Incorporating some form of exercise into your rise routine is a great way to get yourself energized and boost your endorphins. Other ways to feel energized when you rise are taking your shower in the morning, making a cup of coffee you can drink in a mug that has words or phrases that inspire you (for the coffee drinkers!), and/or drinking a big glass of cold water to cleanse your system. If you are seeking a sense of peace in the mornings, you might try a walk outside, yoga, or meditation as part of your routine. Or perhaps, you want to get a head start on your work and info for the day by tackling some work emails, reading news articles, or browsing through your social media.

Let's say you want to rise at 6am (7 hours sleep if you fell asleep about 11pm). Here is a sample Daily Rise Routine that is the companion of the sample Round-Off Routine:
- 6am: Get up (resist the snooze button) & brush my teeth.
- 6:15am: Get on the treadmill. During this time, my partner gets the kids up & dressed.
- 6:35am: Shower & get dressed while my partner gives the kids breakfast & they brush their teeth.
- 7am: Walk kids to the bus stop while talking with them about their day & walk back home.
- 7:20am: Make coffee, eat breakfast, & work on passion goal actions for starting a side business.
- 7:50am: Revisit/edit my daily Commitment Calendar, write down my top 3 goals for the day, words I'm empowering myself with, ways I'm motivating myself, & ways I'm bringing joy into my day.
- 8:10am: Talk with my partner about our plans and goals for the day.
- 8:30am: During my drive to work, listen to an audiobook & drink an 8 oz. bottle of water.

These, of course, are simply sample Rise and Round-Off the Day Routines. Yours has to fit you and what you want. The best way to find out what works is to brainstorm some ideas with allocated times and then try them out. We learn by trying (and failing). By failing, I mean that what you plan may not work out how you anticipate. Things may take longer than you think, it may be harder than you anticipate to rise earlier, or glitches may occur. The first week is always the hardest, and it typically takes at least 21 days of doing the same thing daily to create a habit/routine. You may want to incrementally work toward your new desired sleep and wake times initially, versus jumping right into trying your new times.

You also may want to introduce some aspects of your desired new routines and get them down first before trying all aspects of your routine at once. A routine begins with trial, error, modification, and more modification until you find one that fits great for you. It could be shorter or longer than the sample plans, could include more or less activities, and certainly different activities. But, once you find routines that work, they will get you organized, save you time and energy, give you a feeling of accomplishment, enhance your belief in what you are capable of, and move you closer towards reaching your goals. Now, create and try out your own Rise and Round-Off the Day Routines!

Becoming My Best Self

	Goals & Identity For each area of your life, answer the following questions: *What goals will help me to create a fulfilling life & become my best self?* *By when do I want to achieve each goal?*	**Actions & Habits** For each area of your life, answer the following questions: *What specific actions & habits will move me towards my goals?* *When will I engage in these actions and habits?*
Relationships		
Career		
Financial		
Living Environment		
Community Engagement		

Becoming My Best Self

	Goals & Identity For each area of your life, answer the following questions: *What goals will help me to create a fulfilling life & become my best self?* *By when do I want to achieve each goal?*	**Actions & Habits** For each area of your life, answer the following questions: *What specific actions & habits will move me towards my goals?* *When will I engage in these actions and habits?*
Physical Health		
Mental & Emotional Health		
Intellectual Growth		
Recreation & Relaxation		
Spirituality		

Engage Your Goals!

Week #1

"The only limit to the height of your achievements is the reach of your dreams and your willingness to work for them."
~ Michelle Obama

Revelations From The Research:

Jerabek and Muoio of PsychTests discovered that goal achievers are significantly more likely than non-achievers to visualize themselves successfully accomplishing their goal, plan out how they'll accomplish their goals and overcome obstacles, break down large goals into smaller steps, start goals immediately instead of procrastinating, and keep themselves motivated with small rewards for accomplishing benchmarks on their way to success.[1]

3 Ps Weekly Action Agenda

Week of _____
Date

Professional:

Actions	Complete By

Personal:

Actions	Complete By

Passions:

Actions	Complete By

Longer Term Actions or Projects:

Commitment Calendar

Sunday _____

Date

Time	
5 AM	
6 AM	
7 AM	
8 AM	
9 AM	
10 AM	
11 AM	
12 PM	
1 PM	
2 PM	
3 PM	
4 PM	
5 PM	
6 PM	
7 PM	
8 PM	
9 PM	

Top 3 Goals I'm Setting for Myself Today:
_____
_____
_____

Words & Affirmations I'm Empowering Myself With Today:
_____
_____
_____

Ways I'm Motivating Myself Today:
_____
_____
_____

Ways I'm Bringing Joy into My Day Today:
_____
_____
_____

Monday _____

Date

Time	
5 AM	
6 AM	
7 AM	
8 AM	
9 AM	
10 AM	
11 AM	
12 PM	
1 PM	
2 PM	
3 PM	
4 PM	
5 PM	
6 PM	
7 PM	
8 PM	
9 PM	

Top 3 Goals I'm Setting for Myself Today:
_____
_____
_____

Words & Affirmations I'm Empowering Myself With Today:
_____
_____
_____

Ways I'm Motivating Myself Today:
_____
_____
_____

Ways I'm Bringing Joy into My Day Today:
_____
_____
_____

Tuesday _____
Date

Time	
5 AM	
6 AM	
7 AM	
8 AM	
9 AM	
10 AM	
11 AM	
12 PM	
1 PM	
2 PM	
3 PM	
4 PM	
5 PM	
6 PM	
7 PM	
8 PM	
9 PM	

Top 3 Goals I'm Setting for Myself Today:
_____
_____
_____

Words & Affirmations I'm Empowering Myself With Today:
_____
_____
_____

Ways I'm Motivating Myself Today:
_____
_____
_____

Ways I'm Bringing Joy into My Day Today:
_____
_____
_____

Wednesday _____
Date

Time	
5 AM	
6 AM	
7 AM	
8 AM	
9 AM	
10 AM	
11 AM	
12 PM	
1 PM	
2 PM	
3 PM	
4 PM	
5 PM	
6 PM	
7 PM	
8 PM	
9 PM	

Top 3 Goals I'm Setting for Myself Today:
_____
_____
_____

Words & Affirmations I'm Empowering Myself With Today:
_____
_____
_____

Ways I'm Motivating Myself Today:
_____
_____
_____

Ways I'm Bringing Joy into My Day Today:
_____
_____
_____

Thursday _____
Date

5 AM	**Top 3 Goals I'm Setting for Myself Today:**
6 AM	_____
7 AM	_____
8 AM	_____
9 AM	**Words & Affirmations I'm Empowering Myself With Today:**
10 AM	_____
11 AM	_____
12 PM	_____
1 PM	**Ways I'm Motivating Myself Today:**
2 PM	_____
3 PM	_____
4 PM	_____
5 PM	**Ways I'm Bringing Joy into My Day Today:**
6 PM	_____
7 PM	_____
8 PM	_____
9 PM	

Friday _____
Date

5 AM	**Top 3 Goals I'm Setting for Myself Today:**
6 AM	_____
7 AM	_____
8 AM	_____
9 AM	**Words & Affirmations I'm Empowering Myself With Today:**
10 AM	_____
11 AM	_____
12 PM	_____
1 PM	**Ways I'm Motivating Myself Today:**
2 PM	_____
3 PM	_____
4 PM	_____
5 PM	**Ways I'm Bringing Joy into My Day Today:**
6 PM	_____
7 PM	_____
8 PM	_____
9 PM	

Saturday _____
Date

Time	
5 AM	
6 AM	
7 AM	
8 AM	
9 AM	
10 AM	
11 AM	
12 PM	
1 PM	
2 PM	
3 PM	
4 PM	
5 PM	
6 PM	
7 PM	
8 PM	
9 PM	

Top 3 Goals I'm Setting for Myself Today:
_____
_____
_____

Words & Affirmations I'm Empowering Myself With Today:
_____
_____

Ways I'm Motivating Myself Today:
_____
_____

Ways I'm Bringing Joy into My Day Today:
_____
_____

My Week in Review

Accomplishments I'm Most Proud of This Week:
_____
_____
_____

Obstacles & Challenges I Triumphed Over This Week:
_____
_____
_____

Ways I Was Kind To Myself & Others This Week:
_____
_____
_____

What I'm Most Grateful For This Week:
_____
_____
_____

Engage Your Goals!

Week #2

"The only courage anybody ever needs is the courage to follow your own dreams."
~ Oprah Winfrey

Revelations From The Research:

Wang, Shim, & Wolters discovered that motivational self-talk is correlated with diminished avoidance of challenges and higher goal engagement.[2]

3 Ps Weekly Action Agenda

Week of _____
                            Date

Professional: ## Personal: ## Passions:

Actions   Complete By   Actions   Complete By   Actions   Complete By

Longer Term Actions or Projects:

Commitment Calendar

Sunday _____
Date

Time	
5 AM	
6 AM	
7 AM	
8 AM	
9 AM	
10 AM	
11 AM	
12 PM	
1 PM	
2 PM	
3 PM	
4 PM	
5 PM	
6 PM	
7 PM	
8 PM	
9 PM	

Top 3 Goals I'm Setting for Myself Today:
_____
_____
_____

Words & Affirmations I'm Empowering Myself With Today:
_____
_____
_____

Ways I'm Motivating Myself Today:
_____
_____
_____

Ways I'm Bringing Joy into My Day Today:
_____
_____
_____
_____

Monday _____
Date

Time	
5 AM	
6 AM	
7 AM	
8 AM	
9 AM	
10 AM	
11 AM	
12 PM	
1 PM	
2 PM	
3 PM	
4 PM	
5 PM	
6 PM	
7 PM	
8 PM	
9 PM	

Top 3 Goals I'm Setting for Myself Today:
_____
_____
_____

Words & Affirmations I'm Empowering Myself With Today:
_____
_____
_____

Ways I'm Motivating Myself Today:
_____
_____
_____

Ways I'm Bringing Joy into My Day Today:
_____
_____
_____
_____

Tuesday _____
Date

Time	
5 AM	
6 AM	
7 AM	
8 AM	
9 AM	
10 AM	
11 AM	
12 PM	
1 PM	
2 PM	
3 PM	
4 PM	
5 PM	
6 PM	
7 PM	
8 PM	
9 PM	

Top 3 Goals I'm Setting for Myself Today:
_____
_____
_____

Words & Affirmations I'm Empowering Myself With Today:
_____
_____
_____

Ways I'm Motivating Myself Today:
_____
_____
_____

Ways I'm Bringing Joy into My Day Today:
_____
_____
_____

Wednesday _____
Date

Time	
5 AM	
6 AM	
7 AM	
8 AM	
9 AM	
10 AM	
11 AM	
12 PM	
1 PM	
2 PM	
3 PM	
4 PM	
5 PM	
6 PM	
7 PM	
8 PM	
9 PM	

Top 3 Goals I'm Setting for Myself Today:
_____
_____
_____

Words & Affirmations I'm Empowering Myself With Today:
_____
_____
_____

Ways I'm Motivating Myself Today:
_____
_____
_____

Ways I'm Bringing Joy into My Day Today:
_____
_____
_____

Thursday _____
                                    Date

Time	
5 AM	
6 AM	
7 AM	
8 AM	
9 AM	
10 AM	
11 AM	
12 PM	
1 PM	
2 PM	
3 PM	
4 PM	
5 PM	
6 PM	
7 PM	
8 PM	
9 PM	

Top 3 Goals I'm Setting for Myself Today:
_____
_____
_____

Words & Affirmations I'm Empowering Myself With Today:
_____
_____
_____

Ways I'm Motivating Myself Today:
_____
_____
_____

Ways I'm Bringing Joy into My Day Today:
_____
_____
_____

Friday _____
                                    Date

Time	
5 AM	
6 AM	
7 AM	
8 AM	
9 AM	
10 AM	
11 AM	
12 PM	
1 PM	
2 PM	
3 PM	
4 PM	
5 PM	
6 PM	
7 PM	
8 PM	
9 PM	

Top 3 Goals I'm Setting for Myself Today:
_____
_____
_____

Words & Affirmations I'm Empowering Myself With Today:
_____
_____
_____

Ways I'm Motivating Myself Today:
_____
_____
_____

Ways I'm Bringing Joy into My Day Today:
_____
_____
_____

Saturday _____
Date

Time	
5 AM	
6 AM	
7 AM	
8 AM	
9 AM	
10 AM	
11 AM	
12 PM	
1 PM	
2 PM	
3 PM	
4 PM	
5 PM	
6 PM	
7 PM	
8 PM	
9 PM	

Top 3 Goals I'm Setting for Myself Today:
_____
_____
_____

Words & Affirmations I'm Empowering Myself With Today:
_____
_____
_____

Ways I'm Motivating Myself Today:
_____
_____
_____

Ways I'm Bringing Joy into My Day Today:
_____
_____
_____

My Week in Review

Accomplishments I'm Most Proud of This Week:
_____
_____
_____

Obstacles & Challenges I Triumphed Over This Week:
_____
_____
_____

Ways I Was Kind To Myself & Others This Week:
_____
_____
_____

What I'm Most Grateful For This Week:
_____
_____
_____

Engage Your Goals!

Week #3

"The way to get started is to quit talking and begin doing."
~ Walt Disney

Revelations From The Research:

Locke uncovered that goal commitment and achievement are facilitated by believing in your task-specific capabilities, setting goals that are specific and challenging, and believing the goal is both important as well as attainable.[3]

3 Ps Weekly Action Agenda

Week of _____
Date

Professional:

Actions   Complete By

Personal:

Actions   Complete By

Passions:

Actions   Complete By

Longer Term Actions or Projects:

Commitment Calendar

Sunday _____
Date

Time	
5 AM	
6 AM	
7 AM	
8 AM	
9 AM	
10 AM	
11 AM	
12 PM	
1 PM	
2 PM	
3 PM	
4 PM	
5 PM	
6 PM	
7 PM	
8 PM	
9 PM	

Top 3 Goals I'm Setting for Myself Today:
_____
_____
_____

Words & Affirmations I'm Empowering Myself With Today:
_____
_____
_____

Ways I'm Motivating Myself Today:
_____
_____
_____

Ways I'm Bringing Joy into My Day Today:
_____
_____
_____

Monday _____
Date

Time	
5 AM	
6 AM	
7 AM	
8 AM	
9 AM	
10 AM	
11 AM	
12 PM	
1 PM	
2 PM	
3 PM	
4 PM	
5 PM	
6 PM	
7 PM	
8 PM	
9 PM	

Top 3 Goals I'm Setting for Myself Today:
_____
_____
_____

Words & Affirmations I'm Empowering Myself With Today:
_____
_____
_____

Ways I'm Motivating Myself Today:
_____
_____
_____

Ways I'm Bringing Joy into My Day Today:
_____
_____
_____

Tuesday _____
                                            Date

Time	
5 AM	
6 AM	
7 AM	
8 AM	
9 AM	
10 AM	
11 AM	
12 PM	
1 PM	
2 PM	
3 PM	
4 PM	
5 PM	
6 PM	
7 PM	
8 PM	
9 PM	

Top 3 Goals I'm Setting for Myself Today:
_____
_____
_____

Words & Affirmations I'm Empowering Myself With Today:
_____
_____
_____

Ways I'm Motivating Myself Today:
_____
_____
_____

Ways I'm Bringing Joy into My Day Today:
_____
_____
_____

Wednesday _____
                                            Date

Time	
5 AM	
6 AM	
7 AM	
8 AM	
9 AM	
10 AM	
11 AM	
12 PM	
1 PM	
2 PM	
3 PM	
4 PM	
5 PM	
6 PM	
7 PM	
8 PM	
9 PM	

Top 3 Goals I'm Setting for Myself Today:
_____
_____
_____

Words & Affirmations I'm Empowering Myself With Today:
_____
_____
_____

Ways I'm Motivating Myself Today:
_____
_____
_____

Ways I'm Bringing Joy into My Day Today:
_____
_____
_____

Thursday _____
Date

Time	
5 AM	
6 AM	
7 AM	
8 AM	
9 AM	
10 AM	
11 AM	
12 PM	
1 PM	
2 PM	
3 PM	
4 PM	
5 PM	
6 PM	
7 PM	
8 PM	
9 PM	

Top 3 Goals I'm Setting for Myself Today:
_____
_____
_____

Words & Affirmations I'm Empowering Myself With Today:
_____
_____
_____

Ways I'm Motivating Myself Today:
_____
_____
_____

Ways I'm Bringing Joy into My Day Today:
_____
_____
_____

Friday _____
Date

Time	
5 AM	
6 AM	
7 AM	
8 AM	
9 AM	
10 AM	
11 AM	
12 PM	
1 PM	
2 PM	
3 PM	
4 PM	
5 PM	
6 PM	
7 PM	
8 PM	
9 PM	

Top 3 Goals I'm Setting for Myself Today:
_____
_____
_____

Words & Affirmations I'm Empowering Myself With Today:
_____
_____
_____

Ways I'm Motivating Myself Today:
_____
_____
_____

Ways I'm Bringing Joy into My Day Today:
_____
_____
_____

Saturday _____

Date _____

Time	
5 AM	
6 AM	
7 AM	
8 AM	
9 AM	
10 AM	
11 AM	
12 PM	
1 PM	
2 PM	
3 PM	
4 PM	
5 PM	
6 PM	
7 PM	
8 PM	
9 PM	

Top 3 Goals I'm Setting for Myself Today:
_____
_____
_____

Words & Affirmations I'm Empowering Myself With Today:
_____
_____

Ways I'm Motivating Myself Today:
_____
_____

Ways I'm Bringing Joy into My Day Today:
_____
_____

My Week in Review

Accomplishments I'm Most Proud of This Week:
_____
_____
_____

Obstacles & Challenges I Triumphed Over This Week:
_____
_____
_____

Ways I Was Kind To Myself & Others This Week:
_____
_____
_____

What I'm Most Grateful For This Week:
_____
_____
_____

Engage Your Goals!

Week #4

"The starting point of all achievement is desire."
~ Napoleon Hill

Revelations From The Research:

Powers, Koestner, and Zuroff found that self-criticism is correlated with rumination, procrastinating on goals, and diminished goal progress.[4]

3 Ps Weekly Action Agenda

Week of _____

Date

Professional:

Actions	Complete By

Personal:

Actions	Complete By

Passions:

Actions	Complete By

Longer Term Actions or Projects:

Commitment Calendar

Sunday _____
Date

Time	
5 AM	
6 AM	
7 AM	
8 AM	
9 AM	
10 AM	
11 AM	
12 PM	
1 PM	
2 PM	
3 PM	
4 PM	
5 PM	
6 PM	
7 PM	
8 PM	
9 PM	

Top 3 Goals I'm Setting for Myself Today:
_____
_____
_____

Words & Affirmations I'm Empowering Myself With Today:
_____
_____
_____

Ways I'm Motivating Myself Today:
_____
_____
_____

Ways I'm Bringing Joy into My Day Today:
_____
_____
_____

Monday _____
Date

Time	
5 AM	
6 AM	
7 AM	
8 AM	
9 AM	
10 AM	
11 AM	
12 PM	
1 PM	
2 PM	
3 PM	
4 PM	
5 PM	
6 PM	
7 PM	
8 PM	
9 PM	

Top 3 Goals I'm Setting for Myself Today:
_____
_____
_____

Words & Affirmations I'm Empowering Myself With Today:
_____
_____
_____

Ways I'm Motivating Myself Today:
_____
_____
_____

Ways I'm Bringing Joy into My Day Today:
_____
_____
_____

Tuesday _____
Date

5 AM	
6 AM	
7 AM	
8 AM	
9 AM	
10 AM	
11 AM	
12 PM	
1 PM	
2 PM	
3 PM	
4 PM	
5 PM	
6 PM	
7 PM	
8 PM	
9 PM	

Top 3 Goals I'm Setting for Myself Today:
_____
_____
_____

Words & Affirmations I'm Empowering Myself With Today:
_____
_____
_____

Ways I'm Motivating Myself Today:
_____
_____
_____

Ways I'm Bringing Joy into My Day Today:
_____
_____
_____

Wednesday _____
Date

5 AM	
6 AM	
7 AM	
8 AM	
9 AM	
10 AM	
11 AM	
12 PM	
1 PM	
2 PM	
3 PM	
4 PM	
5 PM	
6 PM	
7 PM	
8 PM	
9 PM	

Top 3 Goals I'm Setting for Myself Today:
_____
_____
_____

Words & Affirmations I'm Empowering Myself With Today:
_____
_____
_____

Ways I'm Motivating Myself Today:
_____
_____
_____

Ways I'm Bringing Joy into My Day Today:
_____
_____
_____

Thursday _____
Date

Time	
5 AM	
6 AM	
7 AM	
8 AM	
9 AM	
10 AM	
11 AM	
12 PM	
1 PM	
2 PM	
3 PM	
4 PM	
5 PM	
6 PM	
7 PM	
8 PM	
9 PM	

Top 3 Goals I'm Setting for Myself Today:
_____
_____
_____

Words & Affirmations I'm Empowering Myself With Today:
_____
_____
_____

Ways I'm Motivating Myself Today:
_____
_____
_____

Ways I'm Bringing Joy into My Day Today:
_____
_____
_____

Friday _____
Date

Time	
5 AM	
6 AM	
7 AM	
8 AM	
9 AM	
10 AM	
11 AM	
12 PM	
1 PM	
2 PM	
3 PM	
4 PM	
5 PM	
6 PM	
7 PM	
8 PM	
9 PM	

Top 3 Goals I'm Setting for Myself Today:
_____
_____
_____

Words & Affirmations I'm Empowering Myself With Today:
_____
_____
_____

Ways I'm Motivating Myself Today:
_____
_____
_____

Ways I'm Bringing Joy into My Day Today:
_____
_____
_____

Saturday _____
Date

Time	
5 AM	
6 AM	
7 AM	
8 AM	
9 AM	
10 AM	
11 AM	
12 PM	
1 PM	
2 PM	
3 PM	
4 PM	
5 PM	
6 PM	
7 PM	
8 PM	
9 PM	

Top 3 Goals I'm Setting for Myself Today:
_____
_____
_____

Words & Affirmations I'm Empowering Myself With Today:
_____
_____
_____

Ways I'm Motivating Myself Today:
_____
_____
_____

Ways I'm Bringing Joy into My Day Today:
_____
_____
_____

My Week in Review

Accomplishments I'm Most Proud of This Week:
_____
_____
_____

Obstacles & Challenges I Triumphed Over This Week:
_____
_____
_____

Ways I Was Kind To Myself & Others This Week:
_____
_____
_____

What I'm Most Grateful For This Week:
_____
_____
_____

Engage Your Goals!

Week #5

"Make the most of yourself by fanning the tiny, inner sparks of possibility into flames of achievement."
~ Golda Meir

Revelations From The Research:

A study by Shahar, Kalnitzki, Shulman, and Blatt discovered that those who are high in self-criticism are less internally motivated toward their goals, make less progress toward their goals, and experience poorer future goal expectations.[5]

3 Ps Weekly Action Agenda

Week of _____
                            Date

Professional: **Personal:**   **Passions:**

Actions   Complete   Actions   Complete   Actions   Complete
               By   By   By

Longer Term Actions or Projects:

Commitment Calendar

Sunday _____

Date

Top 3 Goals I'm Setting for Myself Today:

5 AM
6 AM
7 AM
8 AM
9 AM

Words & Affirmations I'm Empowering Myself With Today:

10 AM
11 AM
12 PM
1 PM

Ways I'm Motivating Myself Today:

2 PM
3 PM
4 PM
5 PM

Ways I'm Bringing Joy into My Day Today:

6 PM
7 PM
8 PM
9 PM

Monday _____

Date

Top 3 Goals I'm Setting for Myself Today:

5 AM
6 AM
7 AM
8 AM
9 AM

Words & Affirmations I'm Empowering Myself With Today:

10 AM
11 AM
12 PM
1 PM

Ways I'm Motivating Myself Today:

2 PM
3 PM
4 PM
5 PM

Ways I'm Bringing Joy into My Day Today:

6 PM
7 PM
8 PM
9 PM

Tuesday _____
Date

5 AM
6 AM
7 AM
8 AM
9 AM
10 AM
11 AM
12 PM
1 PM
2 PM
3 PM
4 PM
5 PM
6 PM
7 PM
8 PM
9 PM

Top 3 Goals I'm Setting for Myself Today:
_____
_____
_____

Words & Affirmations I'm Empowering Myself With Today:
_____
_____
_____

Ways I'm Motivating Myself Today:
_____
_____
_____

Ways I'm Bringing Joy into My Day Today:
_____
_____
_____

Wednesday _____
Date

5 AM
6 AM
7 AM
8 AM
9 AM
10 AM
11 AM
12 PM
1 PM
2 PM
3 PM
4 PM
5 PM
6 PM
7 PM
8 PM
9 PM

Top 3 Goals I'm Setting for Myself Today:
_____
_____
_____

Words & Affirmations I'm Empowering Myself With Today:
_____
_____
_____

Ways I'm Motivating Myself Today:
_____
_____
_____

Ways I'm Bringing Joy into My Day Today:
_____
_____
_____

Thursday _____
                                    Date

5 AM	**Top 3 Goals I'm Setting for Myself Today:**
6 AM	_____
7 AM	_____
8 AM	_____
9 AM	**Words & Affirmations I'm Empowering Myself With Today:**
10 AM	_____
11 AM	_____
12 PM	_____
1 PM	**Ways I'm Motivating Myself Today:**
2 PM	_____
3 PM	_____
4 PM	_____
5 PM	**Ways I'm Bringing Joy into My Day Today:**
6 PM	_____
7 PM	_____
8 PM	_____
9 PM	

Friday _____
                                    Date

5 AM	**Top 3 Goals I'm Setting for Myself Today:**
6 AM	_____
7 AM	_____
8 AM	_____
9 AM	**Words & Affirmations I'm Empowering Myself With Today:**
10 AM	_____
11 AM	_____
12 PM	_____
1 PM	**Ways I'm Motivating Myself Today:**
2 PM	_____
3 PM	_____
4 PM	_____
5 PM	**Ways I'm Bringing Joy into My Day Today:**
6 PM	_____
7 PM	_____
8 PM	_____
9 PM	

Saturday _____

Date

5 AM	**Top 3 Goals I'm Setting for Myself Today:**
6 AM	_____
7 AM	_____
8 AM	_____
9 AM	**Words & Affirmations I'm Empowering Myself With Today:**
10 AM	_____
11 AM	_____
12 PM	_____
1 PM	**Ways I'm Motivating Myself Today:**
2 PM	_____
3 PM	_____
4 PM	_____
5 PM	**Ways I'm Bringing Joy into My Day Today:**
6 PM	_____
7 PM	_____
8 PM	_____
9 PM	

My Week in Review

Accomplishments I'm Most Proud of This Week:
_____
_____
_____

Obstacles & Challenges I Triumphed Over This Week:
_____
_____
_____

Ways I Was Kind To Myself & Others This Week:
_____
_____
_____

What I'm Most Grateful For This Week:
_____
_____
_____

Engage Your Goals!

Week #6

"I didn't get there by wishing for it or hoping for it, but by working for it."
~ Estée Lauder

Revelations From The Research:

Sung discovered that those who use a daily planner to manage their time and goals experience a greater sense of organization, enhanced time management, improved academic performance, and less stress.[6]

3 Ps Weekly Action Agenda

Week of _____
                              Date

Professional:

Actions	Complete By

Personal:

Actions	Complete By

Passions:

Actions	Complete By

Longer Term Actions or Projects:

Commitment Calendar

Sunday _____

Date _____

Top 3 Goals I'm Setting for Myself Today:
_____
_____
_____

Words & Affirmations I'm Empowering Myself With Today:
_____
_____
_____

Ways I'm Motivating Myself Today:
_____
_____
_____

Ways I'm Bringing Joy into My Day Today:
_____
_____
_____

- 5 AM
- 6 AM
- 7 AM
- 8 AM
- 9 AM
- 10 AM
- 11 AM
- 12 PM
- 1 PM
- 2 PM
- 3 PM
- 4 PM
- 5 PM
- 6 PM
- 7 PM
- 8 PM
- 9 PM

Monday _____

Date _____

Top 3 Goals I'm Setting for Myself Today:
_____
_____
_____

Words & Affirmations I'm Empowering Myself With Today:
_____
_____
_____

Ways I'm Motivating Myself Today:
_____
_____
_____

Ways I'm Bringing Joy into My Day Today:
_____
_____
_____

- 5 AM
- 6 AM
- 7 AM
- 8 AM
- 9 AM
- 10 AM
- 11 AM
- 12 PM
- 1 PM
- 2 PM
- 3 PM
- 4 PM
- 5 PM
- 6 PM
- 7 PM
- 8 PM
- 9 PM

Tuesday _____
Date

5 AM	
6 AM	
7 AM	
8 AM	
9 AM	
10 AM	
11 AM	
12 PM	
1 PM	
2 PM	
3 PM	
4 PM	
5 PM	
6 PM	
7 PM	
8 PM	
9 PM	

Top 3 Goals I'm Setting for Myself Today:
_____
_____
_____

Words & Affirmations I'm Empowering Myself With Today:
_____
_____
_____

Ways I'm Motivating Myself Today:
_____
_____
_____

Ways I'm Bringing Joy into My Day Today:
_____
_____
_____

Wednesday _____
Date

5 AM	
6 AM	
7 AM	
8 AM	
9 AM	
10 AM	
11 AM	
12 PM	
1 PM	
2 PM	
3 PM	
4 PM	
5 PM	
6 PM	
7 PM	
8 PM	
9 PM	

Top 3 Goals I'm Setting for Myself Today:
_____
_____
_____

Words & Affirmations I'm Empowering Myself With Today:
_____
_____
_____

Ways I'm Motivating Myself Today:
_____
_____
_____

Ways I'm Bringing Joy into My Day Today:
_____
_____
_____

Thursday _____
Date

5 AM	
6 AM	
7 AM	
8 AM	
9 AM	
10 AM	
11 AM	
12 PM	
1 PM	
2 PM	
3 PM	
4 PM	
5 PM	
6 PM	
7 PM	
8 PM	
9 PM	

Top 3 Goals I'm Setting for Myself Today:
_____
_____
_____

Words & Affirmations I'm Empowering Myself With Today:
_____
_____
_____

Ways I'm Motivating Myself Today:
_____
_____
_____

Ways I'm Bringing Joy into My Day Today:
_____
_____
_____

Friday _____
Date

5 AM	
6 AM	
7 AM	
8 AM	
9 AM	
10 AM	
11 AM	
12 PM	
1 PM	
2 PM	
3 PM	
4 PM	
5 PM	
6 PM	
7 PM	
8 PM	
9 PM	

Top 3 Goals I'm Setting for Myself Today:
_____
_____
_____

Words & Affirmations I'm Empowering Myself With Today:
_____
_____
_____

Ways I'm Motivating Myself Today:
_____
_____
_____

Ways I'm Bringing Joy into My Day Today:
_____
_____
_____

Saturday _____
                              Date

5 AM	Top 3 Goals I'm Setting for Myself Today:
6 AM	_____
7 AM	_____
8 AM	_____
9 AM	Words & Affirmations I'm Empowering Myself With Today:
10 AM	_____
11 AM	_____
12 PM	_____
1 PM	Ways I'm Motivating Myself Today:
2 PM	_____
3 PM	_____
4 PM	_____
5 PM	Ways I'm Bringing Joy into My Day Today:
6 PM	_____
7 PM	_____
8 PM	_____
9 PM	

My Week in Review

Accomplishments I'm Most Proud of This Week:
_____
_____
_____

Obstacles & Challenges I Triumphed Over This Week:
_____
_____
_____

Ways I Was Kind To Myself & Others This Week:
_____
_____
_____

What I'm Most Grateful For This Week:
_____
_____
_____

Engage Your Goals!

Week #7

*"Power's not given to you.
You have to take it."
~ Beyoncé Knowles Carter*

Revelations From The Research:

Brown & Latham found that professionals who set specific, difficult goals have significantly higher task performance at work.[7]

3 Ps Weekly Action Agenda

Week of _____
                            Date

Professional: **Personal:**   **Passions:**

Actions   Complete By   Actions   Complete By   Actions   Complete By

Longer Term Actions or Projects:

Commitment Calendar

Sunday _____
                                        Date

Time	
5 AM	
6 AM	
7 AM	
8 AM	
9 AM	
10 AM	
11 AM	
12 PM	
1 PM	
2 PM	
3 PM	
4 PM	
5 PM	
6 PM	
7 PM	
8 PM	
9 PM	

Top 3 Goals I'm Setting for Myself Today:
_____
_____
_____

Words & Affirmations I'm Empowering Myself With Today:
_____
_____
_____

Ways I'm Motivating Myself Today:
_____
_____
_____

Ways I'm Bringing Joy into My Day Today:
_____
_____
_____

Monday _____
                                        Date

Time	
5 AM	
6 AM	
7 AM	
8 AM	
9 AM	
10 AM	
11 AM	
12 PM	
1 PM	
2 PM	
3 PM	
4 PM	
5 PM	
6 PM	
7 PM	
8 PM	
9 PM	

Top 3 Goals I'm Setting for Myself Today:
_____
_____
_____

Words & Affirmations I'm Empowering Myself With Today:
_____
_____
_____

Ways I'm Motivating Myself Today:
_____
_____
_____

Ways I'm Bringing Joy into My Day Today:
_____
_____
_____

Tuesday _____
Date

5 AM
6 AM
7 AM
8 AM
9 AM
10 AM
11 AM
12 PM
1 PM
2 PM
3 PM
4 PM
5 PM
6 PM
7 PM
8 PM
9 PM

Top 3 Goals I'm Setting for Myself Today:
_____
_____
_____

Words & Affirmations I'm Empowering Myself With Today:
_____
_____
_____

Ways I'm Motivating Myself Today:
_____
_____
_____

Ways I'm Bringing Joy into My Day Today:
_____
_____
_____

Wednesday _____
Date

5 AM
6 AM
7 AM
8 AM
9 AM
10 AM
11 AM
12 PM
1 PM
2 PM
3 PM
4 PM
5 PM
6 PM
7 PM
8 PM
9 PM

Top 3 Goals I'm Setting for Myself Today:
_____
_____
_____

Words & Affirmations I'm Empowering Myself With Today:
_____
_____
_____

Ways I'm Motivating Myself Today:
_____
_____
_____

Ways I'm Bringing Joy into My Day Today:
_____
_____
_____

Thursday _____
Date

Time	
5 AM	
6 AM	
7 AM	
8 AM	
9 AM	
10 AM	
11 AM	
12 PM	
1 PM	
2 PM	
3 PM	
4 PM	
5 PM	
6 PM	
7 PM	
8 PM	
9 PM	

Top 3 Goals I'm Setting for Myself Today:
_____
_____
_____

Words & Affirmations I'm Empowering Myself With Today:
_____
_____
_____

Ways I'm Motivating Myself Today:
_____
_____
_____

Ways I'm Bringing Joy into My Day Today:
_____
_____
_____

Friday _____
Date

Time	
5 AM	
6 AM	
7 AM	
8 AM	
9 AM	
10 AM	
11 AM	
12 PM	
1 PM	
2 PM	
3 PM	
4 PM	
5 PM	
6 PM	
7 PM	
8 PM	
9 PM	

Top 3 Goals I'm Setting for Myself Today:
_____
_____
_____

Words & Affirmations I'm Empowering Myself With Today:
_____
_____
_____

Ways I'm Motivating Myself Today:
_____
_____
_____

Ways I'm Bringing Joy into My Day Today:
_____
_____
_____

Saturday _____
Date

5 AM
6 AM
7 AM
8 AM
9 AM
10 AM
11 AM
12 PM
1 PM
2 PM
3 PM
4 PM
5 PM
6 PM
7 PM
8 PM
9 PM

Top 3 Goals I'm Setting for Myself Today:
_____
_____
_____

Words & Affirmations I'm Empowering Myself With Today:
_____
_____
_____

Ways I'm Motivating Myself Today:
_____
_____
_____

Ways I'm Bringing Joy into My Day Today:
_____
_____
_____

My Week in Review

Accomplishments I'm Most Proud of This Week:
_____
_____
_____
_____

Obstacles & Challenges I Triumphed Over This Week:
_____
_____
_____
_____

Ways I Was Kind To Myself & Others This Week:
_____
_____
_____
_____

What I'm Most Grateful For This Week:
_____
_____
_____
_____

Engage Your Goals!

Week #8

"I'd rather regret the things I've done than Regret the things I haven't done."
~ Lucille Ball

Revelations From The Research:

Kannangara, Allen, Waugh, Nahar, Khan, Rogerson, & Carson found that grit – defined as the combination of passion and sustained persistence toward long-term goal achievement - is correlated with significantly higher levels of self-control, mental well-being, resilience, and a growth-oriented mindset.[8]

3 Ps Weekly Action Agenda

Week of _____
                        Date

Professional: ## Personal: ## Passions:

Actions   Complete   Actions   Complete   Actions   Complete
           By   By   By

Longer Term Actions or Projects:

Commitment Calendar

Sunday _____
Date

Time	
5 AM	
6 AM	
7 AM	
8 AM	
9 AM	
10 AM	
11 AM	
12 PM	
1 PM	
2 PM	
3 PM	
4 PM	
5 PM	
6 PM	
7 PM	
8 PM	
9 PM	

Top 3 Goals I'm Setting for Myself Today:
_____
_____
_____

Words & Affirmations I'm Empowering Myself With Today:
_____
_____
_____

Ways I'm Motivating Myself Today:
_____
_____
_____

Ways I'm Bringing Joy into My Day Today:
_____
_____
_____

Monday _____
Date

Time	
5 AM	
6 AM	
7 AM	
8 AM	
9 AM	
10 AM	
11 AM	
12 PM	
1 PM	
2 PM	
3 PM	
4 PM	
5 PM	
6 PM	
7 PM	
8 PM	
9 PM	

Top 3 Goals I'm Setting for Myself Today:
_____
_____
_____

Words & Affirmations I'm Empowering Myself With Today:
_____
_____
_____

Ways I'm Motivating Myself Today:
_____
_____
_____

Ways I'm Bringing Joy into My Day Today:
_____
_____
_____

Tuesday _____
Date

5 AM	
6 AM	
7 AM	
8 AM	
9 AM	
10 AM	
11 AM	
12 PM	
1 PM	
2 PM	
3 PM	
4 PM	
5 PM	
6 PM	
7 PM	
8 PM	
9 PM	

Top 3 Goals I'm Setting for Myself Today:
_____
_____
_____

Words & Affirmations I'm Empowering Myself With Today:
_____
_____
_____

Ways I'm Motivating Myself Today:
_____
_____
_____

Ways I'm Bringing Joy into My Day Today:
_____
_____
_____

Wednesday _____
Date

5 AM	
6 AM	
7 AM	
8 AM	
9 AM	
10 AM	
11 AM	
12 PM	
1 PM	
2 PM	
3 PM	
4 PM	
5 PM	
6 PM	
7 PM	
8 PM	
9 PM	

Top 3 Goals I'm Setting for Myself Today:
_____
_____
_____

Words & Affirmations I'm Empowering Myself With Today:
_____
_____
_____

Ways I'm Motivating Myself Today:
_____
_____
_____

Ways I'm Bringing Joy into My Day Today:
_____
_____
_____

Thursday _____
                                 Date

Time	
5 AM	
6 AM	
7 AM	
8 AM	
9 AM	
10 AM	
11 AM	
12 PM	
1 PM	
2 PM	
3 PM	
4 PM	
5 PM	
6 PM	
7 PM	
8 PM	
9 PM	

Top 3 Goals I'm Setting for Myself Today:
_____
_____
_____

Words & Affirmations I'm Empowering Myself With Today:
_____
_____
_____

Ways I'm Motivating Myself Today:
_____
_____
_____

Ways I'm Bringing Joy into My Day Today:
_____
_____
_____

Friday _____
                                 Date

Time	
5 AM	
6 AM	
7 AM	
8 AM	
9 AM	
10 AM	
11 AM	
12 PM	
1 PM	
2 PM	
3 PM	
4 PM	
5 PM	
6 PM	
7 PM	
8 PM	
9 PM	

Top 3 Goals I'm Setting for Myself Today:
_____
_____
_____

Words & Affirmations I'm Empowering Myself With Today:
_____
_____
_____

Ways I'm Motivating Myself Today:
_____
_____
_____

Ways I'm Bringing Joy into My Day Today:
_____
_____
_____

Saturday _____
                                              Date

Time	
5 AM	
6 AM	
7 AM	
8 AM	
9 AM	
10 AM	
11 AM	
12 PM	
1 PM	
2 PM	
3 PM	
4 PM	
5 PM	
6 PM	
7 PM	
8 PM	
9 PM	

Top 3 Goals I'm Setting for Myself Today:
_____
_____
_____

Words & Affirmations I'm Empowering Myself With Today:
_____
_____
_____

Ways I'm Motivating Myself Today:
_____
_____
_____

Ways I'm Bringing Joy into My Day Today:
_____
_____
_____

My Week in Review

Accomplishments I'm Most Proud of This Week:
_____
_____
_____

Obstacles & Challenges I Triumphed Over This Week:
_____
_____
_____

Ways I Was Kind To Myself & Others This Week:
_____
_____
_____

What I'm Most Grateful For This Week:
_____
_____
_____

Engage Your Goals!

Week #9

"If you don't like the road you're walking, start paving another one."
~ Dolly Parton

Revelations From The Research:

Bjørnebekk, Gjesme, & Ulriksen found that the motive to achieve success produces positive emotions, satisfaction, and increased performance, whereas the motive to avoid failure creates worry and performance reduction.[9]

3 Ps Weekly Action Agenda

Week of _____
Date

Professional:

Actions	Complete By

Personal:

Actions	Complete By

Passions:

Actions	Complete By

Longer Term Actions or Projects:

Commitment Calendar

Sunday _____

Date

Top 3 Goals I'm Setting for Myself Today:
_____
_____
_____

Words & Affirmations I'm Empowering Myself With Today:
_____
_____
_____

Ways I'm Motivating Myself Today:
_____
_____
_____

Ways I'm Bringing Joy into My Day Today:
_____
_____
_____

5 AM
6 AM
7 AM
8 AM
9 AM
10 AM
11 AM
12 PM
1 PM
2 PM
3 PM
4 PM
5 PM
6 PM
7 PM
8 PM
9 PM

Monday _____

Date

Top 3 Goals I'm Setting for Myself Today:
_____
_____
_____

Words & Affirmations I'm Empowering Myself With Today:
_____
_____
_____

Ways I'm Motivating Myself Today:
_____
_____
_____

Ways I'm Bringing Joy into My Day Today:
_____
_____
_____

5 AM
6 AM
7 AM
8 AM
9 AM
10 AM
11 AM
12 PM
1 PM
2 PM
3 PM
4 PM
5 PM
6 PM
7 PM
8 PM
9 PM

Tuesday _____
Date

5 AM
6 AM
7 AM
8 AM
9 AM
10 AM
11 AM
12 PM
1 PM
2 PM
3 PM
4 PM
5 PM
6 PM
7 PM
8 PM
9 PM

Top 3 Goals I'm Setting for Myself Today:
_____
_____
_____

Words & Affirmations I'm Empowering Myself With Today:
_____
_____
_____

Ways I'm Motivating Myself Today:
_____
_____
_____

Ways I'm Bringing Joy into My Day Today:
_____
_____
_____

Wednesday _____
Date

5 AM
6 AM
7 AM
8 AM
9 AM
10 AM
11 AM
12 PM
1 PM
2 PM
3 PM
4 PM
5 PM
6 PM
7 PM
8 PM
9 PM

Top 3 Goals I'm Setting for Myself Today:
_____
_____
_____

Words & Affirmations I'm Empowering Myself With Today:
_____
_____
_____

Ways I'm Motivating Myself Today:
_____
_____
_____

Ways I'm Bringing Joy into My Day Today:
_____
_____
_____

Thursday _____
Date

- 5 AM
- 6 AM
- 7 AM
- 8 AM
- 9 AM
- 10 AM
- 11 AM
- 12 PM
- 1 PM
- 2 PM
- 3 PM
- 4 PM
- 5 PM
- 6 PM
- 7 PM
- 8 PM
- 9 PM

Top 3 Goals I'm Setting for Myself Today:
_____
_____
_____

Words & Affirmations I'm Empowering Myself With Today:
_____
_____
_____

Ways I'm Motivating Myself Today:
_____
_____
_____

Ways I'm Bringing Joy into My Day Today:
_____
_____
_____
_____

Friday _____
Date

- 5 AM
- 6 AM
- 7 AM
- 8 AM
- 9 AM
- 10 AM
- 11 AM
- 12 PM
- 1 PM
- 2 PM
- 3 PM
- 4 PM
- 5 PM
- 6 PM
- 7 PM
- 8 PM
- 9 PM

Top 3 Goals I'm Setting for Myself Today:
_____
_____
_____

Words & Affirmations I'm Empowering Myself With Today:
_____
_____
_____

Ways I'm Motivating Myself Today:
_____
_____
_____

Ways I'm Bringing Joy into My Day Today:
_____
_____
_____
_____

Saturday _____
                                    Date

Time		
5 AM		**Top 3 Goals I'm Setting for Myself Today:**
6 AM		_____
7 AM		_____
8 AM		_____
9 AM		**Words & Affirmations I'm Empowering Myself With Today:**
10 AM		_____
11 AM		_____
12 PM		_____
1 PM		**Ways I'm Motivating Myself Today:**
2 PM		_____
3 PM		_____
4 PM		_____
5 PM		**Ways I'm Bringing Joy into My Day Today:**
6 PM		_____
7 PM		_____
8 PM		_____
9 PM		

My Week in Review

Accomplishments I'm Most Proud of This Week:
_____
_____
_____

Obstacles & Challenges I Triumphed Over This Week:
_____
_____
_____

Ways I Was Kind To Myself & Others This Week:
_____
_____
_____

What I'm Most Grateful For This Week:
_____
_____
_____

Engage Your Goals!

Week #10

"Step out of the history that is holding you back. Step into the new story you are willing to create."
~ Oprah Winfrey

Revelations From The Research:

Claessens, Van Eerde, Rutte & Roe uncovered that professionals who engage in time management techniques improve their job performance.[10]

3 Ps Weekly Action Agenda

Week of _____
                              Date

Professional:

Actions	Complete By

Personal:

Actions	Complete By

Passions:

Actions	Complete By

Longer Term Actions or Projects:

Commitment Calendar

Sunday _____
Date

Time	
5 AM	
6 AM	
7 AM	
8 AM	
9 AM	
10 AM	
11 AM	
12 PM	
1 PM	
2 PM	
3 PM	
4 PM	
5 PM	
6 PM	
7 PM	
8 PM	
9 PM	

Top 3 Goals I'm Setting for Myself Today:
_____
_____
_____

Words & Affirmations I'm Empowering Myself With Today:
_____
_____
_____

Ways I'm Motivating Myself Today:
_____
_____
_____

Ways I'm Bringing Joy into My Day Today:
_____
_____
_____

Monday _____
Date

Time	
5 AM	
6 AM	
7 AM	
8 AM	
9 AM	
10 AM	
11 AM	
12 PM	
1 PM	
2 PM	
3 PM	
4 PM	
5 PM	
6 PM	
7 PM	
8 PM	
9 PM	

Top 3 Goals I'm Setting for Myself Today:
_____
_____
_____

Words & Affirmations I'm Empowering Myself With Today:
_____
_____
_____

Ways I'm Motivating Myself Today:
_____
_____
_____

Ways I'm Bringing Joy into My Day Today:
_____
_____
_____

Tuesday _____
Date

Time	
5 AM	
6 AM	
7 AM	
8 AM	
9 AM	
10 AM	
11 AM	
12 PM	
1 PM	
2 PM	
3 PM	
4 PM	
5 PM	
6 PM	
7 PM	
8 PM	
9 PM	

Top 3 Goals I'm Setting for Myself Today:
_____
_____
_____

Words & Affirmations I'm Empowering Myself With Today:
_____
_____
_____

Ways I'm Motivating Myself Today:
_____
_____
_____

Ways I'm Bringing Joy into My Day Today:
_____
_____
_____

Wednesday _____
Date

Time	
5 AM	
6 AM	
7 AM	
8 AM	
9 AM	
10 AM	
11 AM	
12 PM	
1 PM	
2 PM	
3 PM	
4 PM	
5 PM	
6 PM	
7 PM	
8 PM	
9 PM	

Top 3 Goals I'm Setting for Myself Today:
_____
_____
_____

Words & Affirmations I'm Empowering Myself With Today:
_____
_____
_____

Ways I'm Motivating Myself Today:
_____
_____
_____

Ways I'm Bringing Joy into My Day Today:
_____
_____
_____

Thursday _____
Date

Time	
5 AM	
6 AM	
7 AM	
8 AM	
9 AM	
10 AM	
11 AM	
12 PM	
1 PM	
2 PM	
3 PM	
4 PM	
5 PM	
6 PM	
7 PM	
8 PM	
9 PM	

Top 3 Goals I'm Setting for Myself Today:
_____
_____
_____

Words & Affirmations I'm Empowering Myself With Today:
_____
_____
_____

Ways I'm Motivating Myself Today:
_____
_____
_____

Ways I'm Bringing Joy into My Day Today:
_____
_____
_____

Friday _____
Date

Time	
5 AM	
6 AM	
7 AM	
8 AM	
9 AM	
10 AM	
11 AM	
12 PM	
1 PM	
2 PM	
3 PM	
4 PM	
5 PM	
6 PM	
7 PM	
8 PM	
9 PM	

Top 3 Goals I'm Setting for Myself Today:
_____
_____
_____

Words & Affirmations I'm Empowering Myself With Today:
_____
_____
_____

Ways I'm Motivating Myself Today:
_____
_____
_____

Ways I'm Bringing Joy into My Day Today:
_____
_____
_____

Saturday _____
                           Date

Time	
5 AM	
6 AM	
7 AM	
8 AM	
9 AM	
10 AM	
11 AM	
12 PM	
1 PM	
2 PM	
3 PM	
4 PM	
5 PM	
6 PM	
7 PM	
8 PM	
9 PM	

Top 3 Goals I'm Setting for Myself Today:
_____
_____
_____

Words & Affirmations I'm Empowering Myself With Today:
_____
_____
_____

Ways I'm Motivating Myself Today:
_____
_____
_____

Ways I'm Bringing Joy into My Day Today:
_____
_____
_____

My Week in Review

Accomplishments I'm Most Proud of This Week:
_____
_____
_____
_____

Obstacles & Challenges I Triumphed Over This Week:
_____
_____
_____
_____

Ways I Was Kind To Myself & Others This Week:
_____
_____
_____
_____

What I'm Most Grateful For This Week:
_____
_____
_____
_____

Engage Your Goals!

Week #11

"I choose to make the rest of my life the best of my life."
~ Louise Hay

Revelations From The Research:

Evans & Hardy conducted a 5-week goal-setting intervention with athletes who had sustained a sports injury and discovered that goal setting was correlated with greater adherence to the rehabilitation program, stronger feelings of self-efficacy, an increase in confidence, and a greater sense of psychological recovery.[11]

3 Ps Weekly Action Agenda

Week of _____
Date

Professional:

Actions   Complete By

Personal:

Actions   Complete By

Passions:

Actions   Complete By

Longer Term Actions or Projects:

Commitment Calendar

Sunday _____
                                                    Date

Time	
5 AM	
6 AM	
7 AM	
8 AM	
9 AM	
10 AM	
11 AM	
12 PM	
1 PM	
2 PM	
3 PM	
4 PM	
5 PM	
6 PM	
7 PM	
8 PM	
9 PM	

Top 3 Goals I'm Setting for Myself Today:
_____
_____
_____

Words & Affirmations I'm Empowering Myself With Today:
_____
_____
_____

Ways I'm Motivating Myself Today:
_____
_____
_____

Ways I'm Bringing Joy into My Day Today:
_____
_____
_____

Monday _____
                                                    Date

Time	
5 AM	
6 AM	
7 AM	
8 AM	
9 AM	
10 AM	
11 AM	
12 PM	
1 PM	
2 PM	
3 PM	
4 PM	
5 PM	
6 PM	
7 PM	
8 PM	
9 PM	

Top 3 Goals I'm Setting for Myself Today:
_____
_____
_____

Words & Affirmations I'm Empowering Myself With Today:
_____
_____
_____

Ways I'm Motivating Myself Today:
_____
_____
_____

Ways I'm Bringing Joy into My Day Today:
_____
_____
_____

Tuesday _____
Date

5 AM	
6 AM	
7 AM	
8 AM	
9 AM	
10 AM	
11 AM	
12 PM	
1 PM	
2 PM	
3 PM	
4 PM	
5 PM	
6 PM	
7 PM	
8 PM	
9 PM	

Top 3 Goals I'm Setting for Myself Today:
_____
_____
_____

Words & Affirmations I'm Empowering Myself With Today:
_____
_____
_____

Ways I'm Motivating Myself Today:
_____
_____
_____

Ways I'm Bringing Joy into My Day Today:
_____
_____
_____

Wednesday _____
Date

5 AM	
6 AM	
7 AM	
8 AM	
9 AM	
10 AM	
11 AM	
12 PM	
1 PM	
2 PM	
3 PM	
4 PM	
5 PM	
6 PM	
7 PM	
8 PM	
9 PM	

Top 3 Goals I'm Setting for Myself Today:
_____
_____
_____

Words & Affirmations I'm Empowering Myself With Today:
_____
_____
_____

Ways I'm Motivating Myself Today:
_____
_____
_____

Ways I'm Bringing Joy into My Day Today:
_____
_____
_____

Thursday _____
Date

Time	
5 AM	
6 AM	
7 AM	
8 AM	
9 AM	
10 AM	
11 AM	
12 PM	
1 PM	
2 PM	
3 PM	
4 PM	
5 PM	
6 PM	
7 PM	
8 PM	
9 PM	

Top 3 Goals I'm Setting for Myself Today:
_____
_____
_____

Words & Affirmations I'm Empowering Myself With Today:
_____
_____
_____

Ways I'm Motivating Myself Today:
_____
_____
_____

Ways I'm Bringing Joy into My Day Today:
_____
_____
_____

Friday _____
Date

Time	
5 AM	
6 AM	
7 AM	
8 AM	
9 AM	
10 AM	
11 AM	
12 PM	
1 PM	
2 PM	
3 PM	
4 PM	
5 PM	
6 PM	
7 PM	
8 PM	
9 PM	

Top 3 Goals I'm Setting for Myself Today:
_____
_____
_____

Words & Affirmations I'm Empowering Myself With Today:
_____
_____
_____

Ways I'm Motivating Myself Today:
_____
_____
_____

Ways I'm Bringing Joy into My Day Today:
_____
_____
_____

Saturday _____
_____ Date

Time	
5 AM	
6 AM	
7 AM	
8 AM	
9 AM	
10 AM	
11 AM	
12 PM	
1 PM	
2 PM	
3 PM	
4 PM	
5 PM	
6 PM	
7 PM	
8 PM	
9 PM	

Top 3 Goals I'm Setting for Myself Today:
_____
_____
_____

Words & Affirmations I'm Empowering Myself With Today:
_____
_____
_____

Ways I'm Motivating Myself Today:
_____
_____
_____

Ways I'm Bringing Joy into My Day Today:
_____
_____
_____

My Week in Review

Accomplishments I'm Most Proud of This Week:
_____
_____
_____

Obstacles & Challenges I Triumphed Over This Week:
_____
_____
_____

Ways I Was Kind To Myself & Others This Week:
_____
_____
_____

What I'm Most Grateful For This Week:
_____
_____
_____

Engage Your Goals!

Week #12

"The question isn't who is going to let me; it's who is going to stop me."
~ Ayn Rand

Revelations From The Research:

Matthews discovered that professionals who write down their goals are 20% more successful in accomplishing them and those who set concrete action plans for their goals and share their progress each week with a supportive friend for accountability purposes are 40% more likely to accomplish their goals.[12]

3 Ps Weekly Action Agenda

Week of _____
                         Date

Professional: ## Personal: ## Passions:

Actions   Complete   Actions   Complete   Actions   Complete
             By   By   By

Longer Term Actions or Projects:

Commitment Calendar

Sunday _____
　　　　　　　　　　　　　　　　　　　　　　Date

- 5 AM
- 6 AM
- 7 AM
- 8 AM
- 9 AM
- 10 AM
- 11 AM
- 12 PM
- 1 PM
- 2 PM
- 3 PM
- 4 PM
- 5 PM
- 6 PM
- 7 PM
- 8 PM
- 9 PM

Top 3 Goals I'm Setting for Myself Today:
_____
_____
_____

Words & Affirmations I'm Empowering Myself With Today:
_____
_____
_____

Ways I'm Motivating Myself Today:
_____
_____
_____

Ways I'm Bringing Joy into My Day Today:
_____
_____
_____

Monday _____
　　　　　　　　　　　　　　　　　　　　　　Date

- 5 AM
- 6 AM
- 7 AM
- 8 AM
- 9 AM
- 10 AM
- 11 AM
- 12 PM
- 1 PM
- 2 PM
- 3 PM
- 4 PM
- 5 PM
- 6 PM
- 7 PM
- 8 PM
- 9 PM

Top 3 Goals I'm Setting for Myself Today:
_____
_____
_____

Words & Affirmations I'm Empowering Myself With Today:
_____
_____
_____

Ways I'm Motivating Myself Today:
_____
_____
_____

Ways I'm Bringing Joy into My Day Today:
_____
_____
_____

Tuesday _____
Date

5 AM	
6 AM	
7 AM	
8 AM	
9 AM	
10 AM	
11 AM	
12 PM	
1 PM	
2 PM	
3 PM	
4 PM	
5 PM	
6 PM	
7 PM	
8 PM	
9 PM	

Top 3 Goals I'm Setting for Myself Today:
_____
_____
_____

Words & Affirmations I'm Empowering Myself With Today:
_____
_____
_____

Ways I'm Motivating Myself Today:
_____
_____
_____

Ways I'm Bringing Joy into My Day Today:
_____
_____
_____

Wednesday _____
Date

5 AM	
6 AM	
7 AM	
8 AM	
9 AM	
10 AM	
11 AM	
12 PM	
1 PM	
2 PM	
3 PM	
4 PM	
5 PM	
6 PM	
7 PM	
8 PM	
9 PM	

Top 3 Goals I'm Setting for Myself Today:
_____
_____
_____

Words & Affirmations I'm Empowering Myself With Today:
_____
_____
_____

Ways I'm Motivating Myself Today:
_____
_____
_____

Ways I'm Bringing Joy into My Day Today:
_____
_____
_____

Thursday _____
Date

Time	
5 AM	
6 AM	
7 AM	
8 AM	
9 AM	
10 AM	
11 AM	
12 PM	
1 PM	
2 PM	
3 PM	
4 PM	
5 PM	
6 PM	
7 PM	
8 PM	
9 PM	

Top 3 Goals I'm Setting for Myself Today:
_____
_____
_____

Words & Affirmations I'm Empowering Myself With Today:
_____
_____
_____

Ways I'm Motivating Myself Today:
_____
_____
_____

Ways I'm Bringing Joy into My Day Today:
_____
_____
_____

Friday _____
Date

Time	
5 AM	
6 AM	
7 AM	
8 AM	
9 AM	
10 AM	
11 AM	
12 PM	
1 PM	
2 PM	
3 PM	
4 PM	
5 PM	
6 PM	
7 PM	
8 PM	
9 PM	

Top 3 Goals I'm Setting for Myself Today:
_____
_____
_____

Words & Affirmations I'm Empowering Myself With Today:
_____
_____
_____

Ways I'm Motivating Myself Today:
_____
_____
_____

Ways I'm Bringing Joy into My Day Today:
_____
_____
_____

Saturday _____
Date

Time	
5 AM	
6 AM	
7 AM	
8 AM	
9 AM	
10 AM	
11 AM	
12 PM	
1 PM	
2 PM	
3 PM	
4 PM	
5 PM	
6 PM	
7 PM	
8 PM	
9 PM	

Top 3 Goals I'm Setting for Myself Today:
_____
_____
_____

Words & Affirmations I'm Empowering Myself With Today:
_____
_____
_____

Ways I'm Motivating Myself Today:
_____
_____
_____

Ways I'm Bringing Joy into My Day Today:
_____
_____
_____

My Week in Review

Accomplishments I'm Most Proud of This Week:
_____
_____
_____
_____

Obstacles & Challenges I Triumphed Over This Week:
_____
_____
_____
_____

Ways I Was Kind To Myself & Others This Week:
_____
_____
_____
_____

What I'm Most Grateful For This Week:
_____
_____
_____
_____

Engage Your Goals!

Week #13

"Change your life today. Don't gamble on the future, act now, without delay."
~ Simone de Beauvoir

Revelations From The Research:

Adams & Jex studied adult professionals taking college courses part-time, having them set goals and priorities, engage in time management strategies, and maintain a system of organization. They found that time management correlates with both health and job satisfaction, as well as perceived control of time and a reduction of work–family conflict.[13]

3 Ps Weekly Action Agenda

Week of _____
Date

Professional: **Personal:**   **Passions:**

Actions	Complete By	Actions	Complete By	Actions	Complete By

Longer Term Actions or Projects:

Commitment Calendar

Sunday _____

Date

5 AM
6 AM
7 AM
8 AM
9 AM
10 AM
11 AM
12 PM
1 PM
2 PM
3 PM
4 PM
5 PM
6 PM
7 PM
8 PM
9 PM

Top 3 Goals I'm Setting for Myself Today:
_____
_____
_____

Words & Affirmations I'm Empowering Myself With Today:
_____
_____
_____

Ways I'm Motivating Myself Today:
_____
_____
_____

Ways I'm Bringing Joy into My Day Today:
_____
_____
_____

Monday _____

Date

5 AM
6 AM
7 AM
8 AM
9 AM
10 AM
11 AM
12 PM
1 PM
2 PM
3 PM
4 PM
5 PM
6 PM
7 PM
8 PM
9 PM

Top 3 Goals I'm Setting for Myself Today:
_____
_____
_____

Words & Affirmations I'm Empowering Myself With Today:
_____
_____
_____

Ways I'm Motivating Myself Today:
_____
_____
_____

Ways I'm Bringing Joy into My Day Today:
_____
_____
_____

Tuesday _____
Date

5 AM
6 AM
7 AM
8 AM
9 AM
10 AM
11 AM
12 PM
1 PM
2 PM
3 PM
4 PM
5 PM
6 PM
7 PM
8 PM
9 PM

Top 3 Goals I'm Setting for Myself Today:
_____
_____
_____

Words & Affirmations I'm Empowering Myself With Today:
_____
_____

Ways I'm Motivating Myself Today:
_____
_____

Ways I'm Bringing Joy into My Day Today:
_____
_____

Wednesday _____
Date

5 AM
6 AM
7 AM
8 AM
9 AM
10 AM
11 AM
12 PM
1 PM
2 PM
3 PM
4 PM
5 PM
6 PM
7 PM
8 PM
9 PM

Top 3 Goals I'm Setting for Myself Today:
_____
_____
_____

Words & Affirmations I'm Empowering Myself With Today:
_____
_____

Ways I'm Motivating Myself Today:
_____
_____

Ways I'm Bringing Joy into My Day Today:
_____
_____

Thursday _____
Date

Time	
5 AM	
6 AM	
7 AM	
8 AM	
9 AM	
10 AM	
11 AM	
12 PM	
1 PM	
2 PM	
3 PM	
4 PM	
5 PM	
6 PM	
7 PM	
8 PM	
9 PM	

Top 3 Goals I'm Setting for Myself Today:
_____
_____
_____

Words & Affirmations I'm Empowering Myself With Today:
_____
_____
_____

Ways I'm Motivating Myself Today:
_____
_____
_____

Ways I'm Bringing Joy into My Day Today:
_____
_____
_____

Friday _____
Date

Time	
5 AM	
6 AM	
7 AM	
8 AM	
9 AM	
10 AM	
11 AM	
12 PM	
1 PM	
2 PM	
3 PM	
4 PM	
5 PM	
6 PM	
7 PM	
8 PM	
9 PM	

Top 3 Goals I'm Setting for Myself Today:
_____
_____
_____

Words & Affirmations I'm Empowering Myself With Today:
_____
_____
_____

Ways I'm Motivating Myself Today:
_____
_____
_____

Ways I'm Bringing Joy into My Day Today:
_____
_____
_____

Saturday _____
                                    Date

Time	
5 AM	
6 AM	
7 AM	
8 AM	
9 AM	
10 AM	
11 AM	
12 PM	
1 PM	
2 PM	
3 PM	
4 PM	
5 PM	
6 PM	
7 PM	
8 PM	
9 PM	

Top 3 Goals I'm Setting for Myself Today:
_____
_____
_____

Words & Affirmations I'm Empowering Myself With Today:
_____
_____
_____

Ways I'm Motivating Myself Today:
_____
_____
_____

Ways I'm Bringing Joy into My Day Today:
_____
_____
_____

My Week in Review

Accomplishments I'm Most Proud of This Week:
_____
_____
_____

Obstacles & Challenges I Triumphed Over This Week:
_____
_____
_____

Ways I Was Kind To Myself & Others This Week:
_____
_____
_____

What I'm Most Grateful For This Week:
_____
_____
_____

Engage Your Goals!

Week #14

"A surplus of effort could overcome a deficit of confidence."
~ Sonia Sotomayor

Revelations From The Research:

Arvey, Dewhirst, & Boling revealed that scientists and engineers who participated in goal clarity planning and goal setting significantly increased their motivation and goal achievement in the workplace, as well as their satisfaction.[14]

3 Ps Weekly Action Agenda

Week of _____
Date

Professional:

Actions   Complete By

Personal:

Actions   Complete By

Passions:

Actions   Complete By

Longer Term Actions or Projects:

Commitment Calendar

Sunday _____
Date

Time	
5 AM	
6 AM	
7 AM	
8 AM	
9 AM	
10 AM	
11 AM	
12 PM	
1 PM	
2 PM	
3 PM	
4 PM	
5 PM	
6 PM	
7 PM	
8 PM	
9 PM	

Top 3 Goals I'm Setting for Myself Today:
_____
_____
_____

Words & Affirmations I'm Empowering Myself With Today:
_____
_____
_____

Ways I'm Motivating Myself Today:
_____
_____
_____

Ways I'm Bringing Joy into My Day Today:
_____
_____
_____

Monday _____
Date

Time	
5 AM	
6 AM	
7 AM	
8 AM	
9 AM	
10 AM	
11 AM	
12 PM	
1 PM	
2 PM	
3 PM	
4 PM	
5 PM	
6 PM	
7 PM	
8 PM	
9 PM	

Top 3 Goals I'm Setting for Myself Today:
_____
_____
_____

Words & Affirmations I'm Empowering Myself With Today:
_____
_____
_____

Ways I'm Motivating Myself Today:
_____
_____
_____

Ways I'm Bringing Joy into My Day Today:
_____
_____
_____

Tuesday _____
                             Date

Time	
5 AM	
6 AM	
7 AM	
8 AM	
9 AM	
10 AM	
11 AM	
12 PM	
1 PM	
2 PM	
3 PM	
4 PM	
5 PM	
6 PM	
7 PM	
8 PM	
9 PM	

Top 3 Goals I'm Setting for Myself Today:
_____
_____
_____

Words & Affirmations I'm Empowering Myself With Today:
_____
_____
_____

Ways I'm Motivating Myself Today:
_____
_____
_____

Ways I'm Bringing Joy into My Day Today:
_____
_____
_____

Wednesday _____
                             Date

Time	
5 AM	
6 AM	
7 AM	
8 AM	
9 AM	
10 AM	
11 AM	
12 PM	
1 PM	
2 PM	
3 PM	
4 PM	
5 PM	
6 PM	
7 PM	
8 PM	
9 PM	

Top 3 Goals I'm Setting for Myself Today:
_____
_____
_____

Words & Affirmations I'm Empowering Myself With Today:
_____
_____
_____

Ways I'm Motivating Myself Today:
_____
_____
_____

Ways I'm Bringing Joy into My Day Today:
_____
_____
_____

Thursday _____
Date

Time	
5 AM	
6 AM	
7 AM	
8 AM	
9 AM	
10 AM	
11 AM	
12 PM	
1 PM	
2 PM	
3 PM	
4 PM	
5 PM	
6 PM	
7 PM	
8 PM	
9 PM	

Top 3 Goals I'm Setting for Myself Today:
_____
_____
_____

Words & Affirmations I'm Empowering Myself With Today:
_____
_____
_____

Ways I'm Motivating Myself Today:
_____
_____
_____

Ways I'm Bringing Joy into My Day Today:
_____
_____
_____

Friday _____
Date

Time	
5 AM	
6 AM	
7 AM	
8 AM	
9 AM	
10 AM	
11 AM	
12 PM	
1 PM	
2 PM	
3 PM	
4 PM	
5 PM	
6 PM	
7 PM	
8 PM	
9 PM	

Top 3 Goals I'm Setting for Myself Today:
_____
_____
_____

Words & Affirmations I'm Empowering Myself With Today:
_____
_____
_____

Ways I'm Motivating Myself Today:
_____
_____
_____

Ways I'm Bringing Joy into My Day Today:
_____
_____
_____

Saturday _____
                           Date

Time	
5 AM	
6 AM	
7 AM	
8 AM	
9 AM	
10 AM	
11 AM	
12 PM	
1 PM	
2 PM	
3 PM	
4 PM	
5 PM	
6 PM	
7 PM	
8 PM	
9 PM	

Top 3 Goals I'm Setting for Myself Today:
_____
_____
_____

Words & Affirmations I'm Empowering Myself With Today:
_____
_____
_____

Ways I'm Motivating Myself Today:
_____
_____
_____

Ways I'm Bringing Joy into My Day Today:
_____
_____
_____

My Week in Review

Accomplishments I'm Most Proud of This Week:
_____
_____
_____
_____

Obstacles & Challenges I Triumphed Over This Week:
_____
_____
_____
_____

Ways I Was Kind To Myself & Others This Week:
_____
_____
_____

What I'm Most Grateful For This Week:
_____
_____
_____
_____

Engage Your Goals!

Week #15

"You can be the lead in your own life."
~ Kerry Washington

Revelations From The Research:

Morisano, Hirsh, Peterson, Pihl & Shore discovered that college students experiencing academic difficulty who participated in a 4-month online goal-setting program displayed significant improvements in academic performance, and through clarifying their goals, they increased their motivation to complete their degrees.[15]

3 Ps Weekly Action Agenda

Week of _____
Date

Professional:

Actions	Complete By

Personal:

Actions	Complete By

Passions:

Actions	Complete By

Longer Term Actions or Projects:

Commitment Calendar

Sunday _____
_____ **Date**

5 AM	**Top 3 Goals I'm Setting for Myself Today:**
6 AM	_____
7 AM	_____
8 AM	_____
9 AM	**Words & Affirmations I'm Empowering Myself With Today:**
10 AM	_____
11 AM	_____
12 PM	_____
1 PM	**Ways I'm Motivating Myself Today:**
2 PM	_____
3 PM	_____
4 PM	_____
5 PM	**Ways I'm Bringing Joy into My Day Today:**
6 PM	_____
7 PM	_____
8 PM	_____
9 PM	

Monday _____
_____ **Date**

5 AM	**Top 3 Goals I'm Setting for Myself Today:**
6 AM	_____
7 AM	_____
8 AM	_____
9 AM	**Words & Affirmations I'm Empowering Myself With Today:**
10 AM	_____
11 AM	_____
12 PM	_____
1 PM	**Ways I'm Motivating Myself Today:**
2 PM	_____
3 PM	_____
4 PM	_____
5 PM	**Ways I'm Bringing Joy into My Day Today:**
6 PM	_____
7 PM	_____
8 PM	_____
9 PM	

Tuesday _____
Date _____

Time	
5 AM	
6 AM	
7 AM	
8 AM	
9 AM	
10 AM	
11 AM	
12 PM	
1 PM	
2 PM	
3 PM	
4 PM	
5 PM	
6 PM	
7 PM	
8 PM	
9 PM	

Top 3 Goals I'm Setting for Myself Today:
_____
_____
_____

Words & Affirmations I'm Empowering Myself With Today:
_____
_____
_____

Ways I'm Motivating Myself Today:
_____
_____
_____

Ways I'm Bringing Joy into My Day Today:
_____
_____
_____

Wednesday _____
Date _____

Time	
5 AM	
6 AM	
7 AM	
8 AM	
9 AM	
10 AM	
11 AM	
12 PM	
1 PM	
2 PM	
3 PM	
4 PM	
5 PM	
6 PM	
7 PM	
8 PM	
9 PM	

Top 3 Goals I'm Setting for Myself Today:
_____
_____
_____

Words & Affirmations I'm Empowering Myself With Today:
_____
_____
_____

Ways I'm Motivating Myself Today:
_____
_____
_____

Ways I'm Bringing Joy into My Day Today:
_____
_____
_____

Thursday _____
Date

- 5 AM
- 6 AM
- 7 AM
- 8 AM
- 9 AM
- 10 AM
- 11 AM
- 12 PM
- 1 PM
- 2 PM
- 3 PM
- 4 PM
- 5 PM
- 6 PM
- 7 PM
- 8 PM
- 9 PM

Top 3 Goals I'm Setting for Myself Today:
_____
_____
_____

Words & Affirmations I'm Empowering Myself With Today:
_____
_____
_____

Ways I'm Motivating Myself Today:
_____
_____
_____

Ways I'm Bringing Joy into My Day Today:
_____
_____
_____

Friday _____
Date

- 5 AM
- 6 AM
- 7 AM
- 8 AM
- 9 AM
- 10 AM
- 11 AM
- 12 PM
- 1 PM
- 2 PM
- 3 PM
- 4 PM
- 5 PM
- 6 PM
- 7 PM
- 8 PM
- 9 PM

Top 3 Goals I'm Setting for Myself Today:
_____
_____
_____

Words & Affirmations I'm Empowering Myself With Today:
_____
_____
_____

Ways I'm Motivating Myself Today:
_____
_____
_____

Ways I'm Bringing Joy into My Day Today:
_____
_____
_____

Saturday _____
Date

5 AM	**Top 3 Goals I'm Setting for Myself Today:**
6 AM	_____
7 AM	_____
8 AM	_____
9 AM	**Words & Affirmations I'm Empowering Myself With Today:**
10 AM	_____
11 AM	_____
12 PM	_____
1 PM	**Ways I'm Motivating Myself Today:**
2 PM	_____
3 PM	_____
4 PM	_____
5 PM	**Ways I'm Bringing Joy into My Day Today:**
6 PM	_____
7 PM	_____
8 PM	_____
9 PM	

My Week in Review

Accomplishments I'm Most Proud of This Week:
_____
_____
_____

Obstacles & Challenges I Triumphed Over This Week:
_____
_____
_____

Ways I Was Kind To Myself & Others This Week:
_____
_____
_____

What I'm Most Grateful For This Week:
_____
_____
_____

Engage Your Goals!

Week #16

"Only put off until tomorrow what you are willing to die having left undone."
~ Pablo Picasso

Revelations From The Research:

Heintzelman & King found that creating environmental structure such as a daily routine has a positive impact on one's sense of meaning in life.[16]

3 Ps Weekly Action Agenda

Week of _____
Date

Professional: **Personal:**   **Passions:**

Actions	Complete By	Actions	Complete By	Actions	Complete By

Longer Term Actions or Projects:

Commitment Calendar

Sunday _____

Date

Time	
5 AM	
6 AM	
7 AM	
8 AM	
9 AM	
10 AM	
11 AM	
12 PM	
1 PM	
2 PM	
3 PM	
4 PM	
5 PM	
6 PM	
7 PM	
8 PM	
9 PM	

Top 3 Goals I'm Setting for Myself Today:
_____
_____
_____

Words & Affirmations I'm Empowering Myself With Today:
_____
_____
_____

Ways I'm Motivating Myself Today:
_____
_____
_____

Ways I'm Bringing Joy into My Day Today:
_____
_____
_____

Monday _____

Date

Time	
5 AM	
6 AM	
7 AM	
8 AM	
9 AM	
10 AM	
11 AM	
12 PM	
1 PM	
2 PM	
3 PM	
4 PM	
5 PM	
6 PM	
7 PM	
8 PM	
9 PM	

Top 3 Goals I'm Setting for Myself Today:
_____
_____
_____

Words & Affirmations I'm Empowering Myself With Today:
_____
_____
_____

Ways I'm Motivating Myself Today:
_____
_____
_____

Ways I'm Bringing Joy into My Day Today:
_____
_____
_____

Tuesday _____
                                    Date

Time	
5 AM	
6 AM	
7 AM	
8 AM	
9 AM	
10 AM	
11 AM	
12 PM	
1 PM	
2 PM	
3 PM	
4 PM	
5 PM	
6 PM	
7 PM	
8 PM	
9 PM	

Top 3 Goals I'm Setting for Myself Today:
_____
_____
_____

Words & Affirmations I'm Empowering Myself With Today:
_____
_____
_____

Ways I'm Motivating Myself Today:
_____
_____
_____

Ways I'm Bringing Joy into My Day Today:
_____
_____
_____

Wednesday _____
                                    Date

Time	
5 AM	
6 AM	
7 AM	
8 AM	
9 AM	
10 AM	
11 AM	
12 PM	
1 PM	
2 PM	
3 PM	
4 PM	
5 PM	
6 PM	
7 PM	
8 PM	
9 PM	

Top 3 Goals I'm Setting for Myself Today:
_____
_____
_____

Words & Affirmations I'm Empowering Myself With Today:
_____
_____
_____

Ways I'm Motivating Myself Today:
_____
_____
_____

Ways I'm Bringing Joy into My Day Today:
_____
_____
_____

Thursday _____
Date

Time	
5 AM	
6 AM	
7 AM	
8 AM	
9 AM	
10 AM	
11 AM	
12 PM	
1 PM	
2 PM	
3 PM	
4 PM	
5 PM	
6 PM	
7 PM	
8 PM	
9 PM	

Top 3 Goals I'm Setting for Myself Today:
_____
_____
_____

Words & Affirmations I'm Empowering Myself With Today:
_____
_____

Ways I'm Motivating Myself Today:
_____
_____

Ways I'm Bringing Joy into My Day Today:
_____
_____
_____

Friday _____
Date

Time	
5 AM	
6 AM	
7 AM	
8 AM	
9 AM	
10 AM	
11 AM	
12 PM	
1 PM	
2 PM	
3 PM	
4 PM	
5 PM	
6 PM	
7 PM	
8 PM	
9 PM	

Top 3 Goals I'm Setting for Myself Today:
_____
_____
_____

Words & Affirmations I'm Empowering Myself With Today:
_____
_____

Ways I'm Motivating Myself Today:
_____
_____

Ways I'm Bringing Joy into My Day Today:
_____
_____
_____

Saturday

_____
Date

Time	
5 AM	
6 AM	
7 AM	
8 AM	
9 AM	
10 AM	
11 AM	
12 PM	
1 PM	
2 PM	
3 PM	
4 PM	
5 PM	
6 PM	
7 PM	
8 PM	
9 PM	

Top 3 Goals I'm Setting for Myself Today:
_____
_____
_____

Words & Affirmations I'm Empowering Myself With Today:
_____
_____
_____

Ways I'm Motivating Myself Today:
_____
_____
_____

Ways I'm Bringing Joy into My Day Today:
_____
_____
_____

My Week in Review

Accomplishments I'm Most Proud of This Week:
_____
_____
_____
_____

Obstacles & Challenges I Triumphed Over This Week:
_____
_____
_____
_____

Ways I Was Kind To Myself & Others This Week:
_____
_____
_____
_____

What I'm Most Grateful For This Week:
_____
_____
_____
_____

Engage Your Goals!

Week #17

"People often say that motivation doesn't last. Well, neither does bathing--that's why we recommend it daily."
~ Zig Ziglar

Revelations From The Research:

Locke, Shaw, Saari, & Latham revealed that in 90% of the goal setting studies they reviewed, setting specific and challenging goals led to higher performance by directing attention, mobilizing effort, increasing persistence, and motivating strategy development.[17]

3 Ps Weekly Action Agenda

Week of _____
Date

Professional: **Personal:**   **Passions:**

Actions	Complete By	Actions	Complete By	Actions	Complete By

Longer Term Actions or Projects:

Commitment Calendar

Sunday _____
                                    Date

Time	
5 AM	
6 AM	
7 AM	
8 AM	
9 AM	
10 AM	
11 AM	
12 PM	
1 PM	
2 PM	
3 PM	
4 PM	
5 PM	
6 PM	
7 PM	
8 PM	
9 PM	

Top 3 Goals I'm Setting for Myself Today:
_____
_____
_____

Words & Affirmations I'm Empowering Myself With Today:
_____
_____
_____

Ways I'm Motivating Myself Today:
_____
_____
_____

Ways I'm Bringing Joy into My Day Today:
_____
_____
_____

Monday _____
                                    Date

Time	
5 AM	
6 AM	
7 AM	
8 AM	
9 AM	
10 AM	
11 AM	
12 PM	
1 PM	
2 PM	
3 PM	
4 PM	
5 PM	
6 PM	
7 PM	
8 PM	
9 PM	

Top 3 Goals I'm Setting for Myself Today:
_____
_____
_____

Words & Affirmations I'm Empowering Myself With Today:
_____
_____
_____

Ways I'm Motivating Myself Today:
_____
_____
_____

Ways I'm Bringing Joy into My Day Today:
_____
_____
_____

Tuesday _____
Date

Time	
5 AM	
6 AM	
7 AM	
8 AM	
9 AM	
10 AM	
11 AM	
12 PM	
1 PM	
2 PM	
3 PM	
4 PM	
5 PM	
6 PM	
7 PM	
8 PM	
9 PM	

Top 3 Goals I'm Setting for Myself Today:
_____
_____
_____

Words & Affirmations I'm Empowering Myself With Today:
_____
_____
_____

Ways I'm Motivating Myself Today:
_____
_____
_____

Ways I'm Bringing Joy into My Day Today:
_____
_____
_____

Wednesday _____
Date

Time	
5 AM	
6 AM	
7 AM	
8 AM	
9 AM	
10 AM	
11 AM	
12 PM	
1 PM	
2 PM	
3 PM	
4 PM	
5 PM	
6 PM	
7 PM	
8 PM	
9 PM	

Top 3 Goals I'm Setting for Myself Today:
_____
_____
_____

Words & Affirmations I'm Empowering Myself With Today:
_____
_____
_____

Ways I'm Motivating Myself Today:
_____
_____
_____

Ways I'm Bringing Joy into My Day Today:
_____
_____
_____

Thursday _____
                                             Date

Time	
5 AM	
6 AM	
7 AM	
8 AM	
9 AM	
10 AM	
11 AM	
12 PM	
1 PM	
2 PM	
3 PM	
4 PM	
5 PM	
6 PM	
7 PM	
8 PM	
9 PM	

Top 3 Goals I'm Setting for Myself Today:
_____
_____
_____

Words & Affirmations I'm Empowering Myself With Today:
_____
_____
_____

Ways I'm Motivating Myself Today:
_____
_____
_____

Ways I'm Bringing Joy into My Day Today:
_____
_____
_____

Friday _____
                                             Date

Time	
5 AM	
6 AM	
7 AM	
8 AM	
9 AM	
10 AM	
11 AM	
12 PM	
1 PM	
2 PM	
3 PM	
4 PM	
5 PM	
6 PM	
7 PM	
8 PM	
9 PM	

Top 3 Goals I'm Setting for Myself Today:
_____
_____
_____

Words & Affirmations I'm Empowering Myself With Today:
_____
_____
_____

Ways I'm Motivating Myself Today:
_____
_____
_____

Ways I'm Bringing Joy into My Day Today:
_____
_____
_____

Saturday _____
Date

Time	
5 AM	
6 AM	
7 AM	
8 AM	
9 AM	
10 AM	
11 AM	
12 PM	
1 PM	
2 PM	
3 PM	
4 PM	
5 PM	
6 PM	
7 PM	
8 PM	
9 PM	

Top 3 Goals I'm Setting for Myself Today:
_____
_____
_____

Words & Affirmations I'm Empowering Myself With Today:
_____
_____
_____

Ways I'm Motivating Myself Today:
_____
_____
_____

Ways I'm Bringing Joy into My Day Today:
_____
_____
_____

My Week in Review

Accomplishments I'm Most Proud of This Week:
_____
_____
_____

Obstacles & Challenges I Triumphed Over This Week:
_____
_____
_____

Ways I Was Kind To Myself & Others This Week:
_____
_____
_____

What I'm Most Grateful For This Week:
_____
_____
_____

Engage Your Goals!

Week #18

"The only place where success comes before work is in the dictionary."
~ Vidal Sassoon

Revelations From The Research:

Wu, Matthews, & Dagher studied entrepreneurs and found that when they remained persistent in setting goals it propelled their business success. Furthermore, the study discovered that breaking down complex goals into easier to manage steps made entrepreneurs significantly more likely to complete the goals they set.[18]

3 Ps Weekly Action Agenda

Week of _____
                      Date

Professional: **Personal:**   **Passions:**

Actions   Complete   Actions   Complete   Actions   Complete
           By   By   By

Longer Term Actions or Projects:

Commitment Calendar

Sunday _____

Date _____

Time	
5 AM	
6 AM	
7 AM	
8 AM	
9 AM	
10 AM	
11 AM	
12 PM	
1 PM	
2 PM	
3 PM	
4 PM	
5 PM	
6 PM	
7 PM	
8 PM	
9 PM	

Top 3 Goals I'm Setting for Myself Today:
_____
_____
_____

Words & Affirmations I'm Empowering Myself With Today:
_____
_____
_____

Ways I'm Motivating Myself Today:
_____
_____
_____

Ways I'm Bringing Joy into My Day Today:
_____
_____
_____

Monday _____

Date _____

Time	
5 AM	
6 AM	
7 AM	
8 AM	
9 AM	
10 AM	
11 AM	
12 PM	
1 PM	
2 PM	
3 PM	
4 PM	
5 PM	
6 PM	
7 PM	
8 PM	
9 PM	

Top 3 Goals I'm Setting for Myself Today:
_____
_____
_____

Words & Affirmations I'm Empowering Myself With Today:
_____
_____
_____

Ways I'm Motivating Myself Today:
_____
_____
_____

Ways I'm Bringing Joy into My Day Today:
_____
_____
_____

Tuesday _____
Date

5 AM
6 AM
7 AM
8 AM
9 AM
10 AM
11 AM
12 PM
1 PM
2 PM
3 PM
4 PM
5 PM
6 PM
7 PM
8 PM
9 PM

Top 3 Goals I'm Setting for Myself Today:

Words & Affirmations I'm Empowering Myself With Today:

Ways I'm Motivating Myself Today:

Ways I'm Bringing Joy into My Day Today:

Wednesday _____
Date

5 AM
6 AM
7 AM
8 AM
9 AM
10 AM
11 AM
12 PM
1 PM
2 PM
3 PM
4 PM
5 PM
6 PM
7 PM
8 PM
9 PM

Top 3 Goals I'm Setting for Myself Today:

Words & Affirmations I'm Empowering Myself With Today:

Ways I'm Motivating Myself Today:

Ways I'm Bringing Joy into My Day Today:

Thursday _____
Date

Time		
5 AM		**Top 3 Goals I'm Setting for Myself Today:**
6 AM		_____
7 AM		_____
8 AM		_____
9 AM		**Words & Affirmations I'm Empowering Myself With Today:**
10 AM		_____
11 AM		_____
12 PM		_____
1 PM		**Ways I'm Motivating Myself Today:**
2 PM		_____
3 PM		_____
4 PM		_____
5 PM		**Ways I'm Bringing Joy into My Day Today:**
6 PM		_____
7 PM		_____
8 PM		_____
9 PM		

Friday _____
Date

Time		
5 AM		**Top 3 Goals I'm Setting for Myself Today:**
6 AM		_____
7 AM		_____
8 AM		_____
9 AM		**Words & Affirmations I'm Empowering Myself With Today:**
10 AM		_____
11 AM		_____
12 PM		_____
1 PM		**Ways I'm Motivating Myself Today:**
2 PM		_____
3 PM		_____
4 PM		_____
5 PM		**Ways I'm Bringing Joy into My Day Today:**
6 PM		_____
7 PM		_____
8 PM		_____
9 PM		

Saturday _____
Date

Time	
5 AM	
6 AM	
7 AM	
8 AM	
9 AM	
10 AM	
11 AM	
12 PM	
1 PM	
2 PM	
3 PM	
4 PM	
5 PM	
6 PM	
7 PM	
8 PM	
9 PM	

Top 3 Goals I'm Setting for Myself Today:
_____
_____
_____

Words & Affirmations I'm Empowering Myself With Today:
_____
_____
_____

Ways I'm Motivating Myself Today:
_____
_____
_____

Ways I'm Bringing Joy into My Day Today:
_____
_____
_____

My Week in Review

Accomplishments I'm Most Proud of This Week:
_____
_____
_____
_____

Obstacles & Challenges I Triumphed Over This Week:
_____
_____
_____
_____

Ways I Was Kind To Myself & Others This Week:
_____
_____
_____
_____

What I'm Most Grateful For This Week:
_____
_____
_____
_____

Engage Your Goals!

Week #19

"Normal is not something to aspire to, it's something to get away from."
~ Jodie Foster

Revelations From The Research:

Wang, Kao, Huan, & Wu discovered that those who apply time management techniques to effectively manage their free time experienced a better quality of life.[19]

3 Ps Weekly Action Agenda

Week of _____
Date

Professional:

Actions   Complete By

Personal:

Actions   Complete By

Passions:

Actions   Complete By

Longer Term Actions or Projects:

Commitment Calendar

Sunday _____
                                    Date

Time	
5 AM	
6 AM	
7 AM	
8 AM	
9 AM	
10 AM	
11 AM	
12 PM	
1 PM	
2 PM	
3 PM	
4 PM	
5 PM	
6 PM	
7 PM	
8 PM	
9 PM	

Top 3 Goals I'm Setting for Myself Today:
_____
_____
_____

Words & Affirmations I'm Empowering Myself With Today:
_____
_____
_____

Ways I'm Motivating Myself Today:
_____
_____
_____

Ways I'm Bringing Joy into My Day Today:
_____
_____
_____

Monday _____
                                    Date

Time	
5 AM	
6 AM	
7 AM	
8 AM	
9 AM	
10 AM	
11 AM	
12 PM	
1 PM	
2 PM	
3 PM	
4 PM	
5 PM	
6 PM	
7 PM	
8 PM	
9 PM	

Top 3 Goals I'm Setting for Myself Today:
_____
_____
_____

Words & Affirmations I'm Empowering Myself With Today:
_____
_____
_____

Ways I'm Motivating Myself Today:
_____
_____
_____

Ways I'm Bringing Joy into My Day Today:
_____
_____
_____

Tuesday _____
Date

5 AM	
6 AM	
7 AM	
8 AM	
9 AM	
10 AM	
11 AM	
12 PM	
1 PM	
2 PM	
3 PM	
4 PM	
5 PM	
6 PM	
7 PM	
8 PM	
9 PM	

Top 3 Goals I'm Setting for Myself Today:
_____
_____
_____

Words & Affirmations I'm Empowering Myself With Today:
_____
_____
_____

Ways I'm Motivating Myself Today:
_____
_____
_____

Ways I'm Bringing Joy into My Day Today:
_____
_____
_____

Wednesday _____
Date

5 AM	
6 AM	
7 AM	
8 AM	
9 AM	
10 AM	
11 AM	
12 PM	
1 PM	
2 PM	
3 PM	
4 PM	
5 PM	
6 PM	
7 PM	
8 PM	
9 PM	

Top 3 Goals I'm Setting for Myself Today:
_____
_____
_____

Words & Affirmations I'm Empowering Myself With Today:
_____
_____
_____

Ways I'm Motivating Myself Today:
_____
_____
_____

Ways I'm Bringing Joy into My Day Today:
_____
_____
_____

Thursday _____
Date

Time	
5 AM	
6 AM	
7 AM	
8 AM	
9 AM	
10 AM	
11 AM	
12 PM	
1 PM	
2 PM	
3 PM	
4 PM	
5 PM	
6 PM	
7 PM	
8 PM	
9 PM	

Top 3 Goals I'm Setting for Myself Today:
_____
_____
_____

Words & Affirmations I'm Empowering Myself With Today:
_____
_____
_____

Ways I'm Motivating Myself Today:
_____
_____
_____

Ways I'm Bringing Joy into My Day Today:
_____
_____
_____

Friday _____
Date

Time	
5 AM	
6 AM	
7 AM	
8 AM	
9 AM	
10 AM	
11 AM	
12 PM	
1 PM	
2 PM	
3 PM	
4 PM	
5 PM	
6 PM	
7 PM	
8 PM	
9 PM	

Top 3 Goals I'm Setting for Myself Today:
_____
_____
_____

Words & Affirmations I'm Empowering Myself With Today:
_____
_____
_____

Ways I'm Motivating Myself Today:
_____
_____
_____

Ways I'm Bringing Joy into My Day Today:
_____
_____
_____

Saturday _____
Date

Time	
5 AM	
6 AM	
7 AM	
8 AM	
9 AM	
10 AM	
11 AM	
12 PM	
1 PM	
2 PM	
3 PM	
4 PM	
5 PM	
6 PM	
7 PM	
8 PM	
9 PM	

Top 3 Goals I'm Setting for Myself Today:
_____
_____
_____

Words & Affirmations I'm Empowering Myself With Today:
_____
_____
_____

Ways I'm Motivating Myself Today:
_____
_____
_____

Ways I'm Bringing Joy into My Day Today:
_____
_____
_____

My Week in Review

Accomplishments I'm Most Proud of This Week:
_____
_____
_____
_____

Obstacles & Challenges I Triumphed Over This Week:
_____
_____
_____
_____

Ways I Was Kind To Myself & Others This Week:
_____
_____
_____
_____

What I'm Most Grateful For This Week:
_____
_____
_____
_____

Engage Your Goals!

Week #20

"I do not try to dance better than anyone else. I only try to dance better than myself."
~ Arianna Huffington

Revelations From The Research:

Annesi led a study of adult members of fitness club who had previously done no regular exercise within the last 6 months. They had participants generate several one-year exercise-related goals and rate their success in attaining these goals. Participants then broke each long-term goal down into a 6-week short-term. They discovered that those who set long-term goals and broke them down into short-term goals had significantly better exercise attendance and perseverance.[20]

3 Ps Weekly Action Agenda

Week of _____
Date

Professional: **Personal:**   **Passions:**

Actions   Complete By   Actions   Complete By   Actions   Complete By

Longer Term Actions or Projects:

Commitment Calendar

Sunday _____
Date

Time	
5 AM	
6 AM	
7 AM	
8 AM	
9 AM	
10 AM	
11 AM	
12 PM	
1 PM	
2 PM	
3 PM	
4 PM	
5 PM	
6 PM	
7 PM	
8 PM	
9 PM	

Top 3 Goals I'm Setting for Myself Today:
_____
_____
_____

Words & Affirmations I'm Empowering Myself With Today:
_____
_____
_____

Ways I'm Motivating Myself Today:
_____
_____
_____

Ways I'm Bringing Joy into My Day Today:
_____
_____
_____

Monday _____
Date

Time	
5 AM	
6 AM	
7 AM	
8 AM	
9 AM	
10 AM	
11 AM	
12 PM	
1 PM	
2 PM	
3 PM	
4 PM	
5 PM	
6 PM	
7 PM	
8 PM	
9 PM	

Top 3 Goals I'm Setting for Myself Today:
_____
_____
_____

Words & Affirmations I'm Empowering Myself With Today:
_____
_____
_____

Ways I'm Motivating Myself Today:
_____
_____
_____

Ways I'm Bringing Joy into My Day Today:
_____
_____
_____

Tuesday _____
Date

5 AM
6 AM
7 AM
8 AM
9 AM
10 AM
11 AM
12 PM
1 PM
2 PM
3 PM
4 PM
5 PM
6 PM
7 PM
8 PM
9 PM

Top 3 Goals I'm Setting for Myself Today:
_____
_____
_____

Words & Affirmations I'm Empowering Myself With Today:
_____
_____
_____

Ways I'm Motivating Myself Today:
_____
_____
_____

Ways I'm Bringing Joy into My Day Today:
_____
_____
_____

Wednesday _____
Date

5 AM
6 AM
7 AM
8 AM
9 AM
10 AM
11 AM
12 PM
1 PM
2 PM
3 PM
4 PM
5 PM
6 PM
7 PM
8 PM
9 PM

Top 3 Goals I'm Setting for Myself Today:
_____
_____
_____

Words & Affirmations I'm Empowering Myself With Today:
_____
_____
_____

Ways I'm Motivating Myself Today:
_____
_____
_____

Ways I'm Bringing Joy into My Day Today:
_____
_____
_____

Thursday _____
Date

Time	
5 AM	
6 AM	
7 AM	
8 AM	
9 AM	
10 AM	
11 AM	
12 PM	
1 PM	
2 PM	
3 PM	
4 PM	
5 PM	
6 PM	
7 PM	
8 PM	
9 PM	

Top 3 Goals I'm Setting for Myself Today:
_____
_____
_____

Words & Affirmations I'm Empowering Myself With Today:
_____
_____
_____

Ways I'm Motivating Myself Today:
_____
_____
_____

Ways I'm Bringing Joy into My Day Today:
_____
_____
_____

Friday _____
Date

Time	
5 AM	
6 AM	
7 AM	
8 AM	
9 AM	
10 AM	
11 AM	
12 PM	
1 PM	
2 PM	
3 PM	
4 PM	
5 PM	
6 PM	
7 PM	
8 PM	
9 PM	

Top 3 Goals I'm Setting for Myself Today:
_____
_____
_____

Words & Affirmations I'm Empowering Myself With Today:
_____
_____
_____

Ways I'm Motivating Myself Today:
_____
_____
_____

Ways I'm Bringing Joy into My Day Today:
_____
_____
_____

Saturday _____
                                    Date

Time	
5 AM	
6 AM	
7 AM	
8 AM	
9 AM	
10 AM	
11 AM	
12 PM	
1 PM	
2 PM	
3 PM	
4 PM	
5 PM	
6 PM	
7 PM	
8 PM	
9 PM	

Top 3 Goals I'm Setting for Myself Today:
_____
_____
_____

Words & Affirmations I'm Empowering Myself With Today:
_____
_____
_____

Ways I'm Motivating Myself Today:
_____
_____
_____

Ways I'm Bringing Joy into My Day Today:
_____
_____
_____

My Week in Review

Accomplishments I'm Most Proud of This Week:
_____
_____
_____

Obstacles & Challenges I Triumphed Over This Week:
_____
_____
_____

Ways I Was Kind To Myself & Others This Week:
_____
_____
_____

What I'm Most Grateful For This Week:
_____
_____
_____

Engage Your Goals!

Week #21

*"I'm always perpetually out of
my comfort zone."
~ Tory Burch*

Revelations From The Research:

McMillan uncovered that goal-setting strategies help kids improve their math achievement, reading comprehension, and motivation towards academic work.[21]

3 Ps Weekly Action Agenda

Week of _____
                      Date

Professional:		**Personal:**		**Passions:**	
Actions	Complete By	Actions	Complete By	Actions	Complete By

Longer Term Actions or Projects:

Commitment Calendar

Sunday _____
Date

Time	
5 AM	
6 AM	
7 AM	
8 AM	
9 AM	
10 AM	
11 AM	
12 PM	
1 PM	
2 PM	
3 PM	
4 PM	
5 PM	
6 PM	
7 PM	
8 PM	
9 PM	

Top 3 Goals I'm Setting for Myself Today:
_____
_____
_____

Words & Affirmations I'm Empowering Myself With Today:
_____
_____
_____

Ways I'm Motivating Myself Today:
_____
_____
_____

Ways I'm Bringing Joy into My Day Today:
_____
_____
_____

Monday _____
Date

Time	
5 AM	
6 AM	
7 AM	
8 AM	
9 AM	
10 AM	
11 AM	
12 PM	
1 PM	
2 PM	
3 PM	
4 PM	
5 PM	
6 PM	
7 PM	
8 PM	
9 PM	

Top 3 Goals I'm Setting for Myself Today:
_____
_____
_____

Words & Affirmations I'm Empowering Myself With Today:
_____
_____
_____

Ways I'm Motivating Myself Today:
_____
_____
_____

Ways I'm Bringing Joy into My Day Today:
_____
_____
_____

Tuesday _____
Date

5 AM
6 AM
7 AM
8 AM
9 AM
10 AM
11 AM
12 PM
1 PM
2 PM
3 PM
4 PM
5 PM
6 PM
7 PM
8 PM
9 PM

Top 3 Goals I'm Setting for Myself Today:
_____
_____
_____

Words & Affirmations I'm Empowering Myself With Today:
_____
_____
_____

Ways I'm Motivating Myself Today:
_____
_____
_____

Ways I'm Bringing Joy into My Day Today:
_____
_____
_____

Wednesday _____
Date

5 AM
6 AM
7 AM
8 AM
9 AM
10 AM
11 AM
12 PM
1 PM
2 PM
3 PM
4 PM
5 PM
6 PM
7 PM
8 PM
9 PM

Top 3 Goals I'm Setting for Myself Today:
_____
_____
_____

Words & Affirmations I'm Empowering Myself With Today:
_____
_____
_____

Ways I'm Motivating Myself Today:
_____
_____
_____

Ways I'm Bringing Joy into My Day Today:
_____
_____
_____

Thursday _____
Date

5 AM	
6 AM	
7 AM	
8 AM	
9 AM	
10 AM	
11 AM	
12 PM	
1 PM	
2 PM	
3 PM	
4 PM	
5 PM	
6 PM	
7 PM	
8 PM	
9 PM	

Top 3 Goals I'm Setting for Myself Today:
_____
_____
_____

Words & Affirmations I'm Empowering Myself With Today:
_____
_____
_____

Ways I'm Motivating Myself Today:
_____
_____
_____

Ways I'm Bringing Joy into My Day Today:
_____
_____
_____

Friday _____
Date

5 AM	
6 AM	
7 AM	
8 AM	
9 AM	
10 AM	
11 AM	
12 PM	
1 PM	
2 PM	
3 PM	
4 PM	
5 PM	
6 PM	
7 PM	
8 PM	
9 PM	

Top 3 Goals I'm Setting for Myself Today:
_____
_____
_____

Words & Affirmations I'm Empowering Myself With Today:
_____
_____
_____

Ways I'm Motivating Myself Today:
_____
_____
_____

Ways I'm Bringing Joy into My Day Today:
_____
_____
_____

Saturday _____
Date

5 AM
6 AM
7 AM
8 AM
9 AM
10 AM
11 AM
12 PM
1 PM
2 PM
3 PM
4 PM
5 PM
6 PM
7 PM
8 PM
9 PM

Top 3 Goals I'm Setting for Myself Today:
_____
_____
_____

Words & Affirmations I'm Empowering Myself With Today:
_____
_____
_____

Ways I'm Motivating Myself Today:
_____
_____
_____

Ways I'm Bringing Joy into My Day Today:
_____
_____
_____

My Week in Review

Accomplishments I'm Most Proud of This Week:
_____
_____
_____

Obstacles & Challenges I Triumphed Over This Week:
_____
_____
_____

Ways I Was Kind To Myself & Others This Week:
_____
_____
_____

What I'm Most Grateful For This Week:
_____
_____
_____

Engage Your Goals!

Week #22

"If you can't go straight ahead, you go around the corner."
~ Cher

Revelations From The Research:

Barrett, Savage, & Ades conducted a study with cardiac rehabilitation patients and found that those who established a specific weight loss goal and attended behavioral weight loss training sessions lost more weight.[22]

3 Ps Weekly Action Agenda

Week of _____
         Date

Professional:

Actions   Complete By

Personal:

Actions   Complete By

Passions:

Actions   Complete By

Longer Term Actions or Projects:

Commitment Calendar

Sunday _____

Date

5 AM
6 AM
7 AM
8 AM
9 AM
10 AM
11 AM
12 PM
1 PM
2 PM
3 PM
4 PM
5 PM
6 PM
7 PM
8 PM
9 PM

Top 3 Goals I'm Setting for Myself Today:
_____
_____
_____

Words & Affirmations I'm Empowering Myself With Today:
_____
_____
_____

Ways I'm Motivating Myself Today:
_____
_____
_____

Ways I'm Bringing Joy into My Day Today:
_____
_____
_____

Monday _____

Date

5 AM
6 AM
7 AM
8 AM
9 AM
10 AM
11 AM
12 PM
1 PM
2 PM
3 PM
4 PM
5 PM
6 PM
7 PM
8 PM
9 PM

Top 3 Goals I'm Setting for Myself Today:
_____
_____
_____

Words & Affirmations I'm Empowering Myself With Today:
_____
_____
_____

Ways I'm Motivating Myself Today:
_____
_____
_____

Ways I'm Bringing Joy into My Day Today:
_____
_____
_____

Tuesday _____
Date

5 AM	
6 AM	
7 AM	
8 AM	
9 AM	
10 AM	
11 AM	
12 PM	
1 PM	
2 PM	
3 PM	
4 PM	
5 PM	
6 PM	
7 PM	
8 PM	
9 PM	

Top 3 Goals I'm Setting for Myself Today:
_____
_____
_____

Words & Affirmations I'm Empowering Myself With Today:
_____
_____
_____

Ways I'm Motivating Myself Today:
_____
_____
_____

Ways I'm Bringing Joy into My Day Today:
_____
_____
_____

Wednesday _____
Date

5 AM	
6 AM	
7 AM	
8 AM	
9 AM	
10 AM	
11 AM	
12 PM	
1 PM	
2 PM	
3 PM	
4 PM	
5 PM	
6 PM	
7 PM	
8 PM	
9 PM	

Top 3 Goals I'm Setting for Myself Today:
_____
_____
_____

Words & Affirmations I'm Empowering Myself With Today:
_____
_____
_____

Ways I'm Motivating Myself Today:
_____
_____
_____

Ways I'm Bringing Joy into My Day Today:
_____
_____
_____

Thursday _____
Date

5 AM	
6 AM	
7 AM	
8 AM	
9 AM	
10 AM	
11 AM	
12 PM	
1 PM	
2 PM	
3 PM	
4 PM	
5 PM	
6 PM	
7 PM	
8 PM	
9 PM	

Top 3 Goals I'm Setting for Myself Today:
_____
_____
_____

Words & Affirmations I'm Empowering Myself With Today:
_____
_____

Ways I'm Motivating Myself Today:
_____
_____

Ways I'm Bringing Joy into My Day Today:
_____
_____
_____

Friday _____
Date

5 AM	
6 AM	
7 AM	
8 AM	
9 AM	
10 AM	
11 AM	
12 PM	
1 PM	
2 PM	
3 PM	
4 PM	
5 PM	
6 PM	
7 PM	
8 PM	
9 PM	

Top 3 Goals I'm Setting for Myself Today:
_____
_____
_____

Words & Affirmations I'm Empowering Myself With Today:
_____
_____

Ways I'm Motivating Myself Today:
_____
_____

Ways I'm Bringing Joy into My Day Today:
_____
_____
_____

Saturday _____
                                    Date

5 AM	**Top 3 Goals I'm Setting for Myself Today:**
6 AM	_____
7 AM	_____
8 AM	_____
9 AM	**Words & Affirmations I'm Empowering Myself With Today:**
10 AM	_____
11 AM	_____
12 PM	_____
1 PM	**Ways I'm Motivating Myself Today:**
2 PM	_____
3 PM	_____
4 PM	_____
5 PM	**Ways I'm Bringing Joy into My Day Today:**
6 PM	_____
7 PM	_____
8 PM	_____
9 PM	

My Week in Review

Accomplishments I'm Most Proud of This Week:
_____
_____
_____

Obstacles & Challenges I Triumphed Over This Week:
_____
_____
_____

Ways I Was Kind To Myself & Others This Week:
_____
_____
_____

What I'm Most Grateful For This Week:
_____
_____
_____

Engage Your Goals!

Week #23

"Too many of us are not living our dreams because we are living our fears."
~ Les Brown

Revelations From The Research:

Becker conducted a study of families, asking them to set goals related to reducing their residential energy consumption. They found that the families who set the most difficult goals conserved the most energy.[23]

3 Ps Weekly Action Agenda

Week of _____

Date

Professional:

Actions   Complete By

Personal:

Actions   Complete By

Passions:

Actions   Complete By

Longer Term Actions or Projects:

Commitment Calendar

Sunday _____
                                    Date

Time	
5 AM	
6 AM	
7 AM	
8 AM	
9 AM	
10 AM	
11 AM	
12 PM	
1 PM	
2 PM	
3 PM	
4 PM	
5 PM	
6 PM	
7 PM	
8 PM	
9 PM	

Top 3 Goals I'm Setting for Myself Today:
_____
_____
_____

Words & Affirmations I'm Empowering Myself With Today:
_____
_____
_____

Ways I'm Motivating Myself Today:
_____
_____
_____

Ways I'm Bringing Joy into My Day Today:
_____
_____
_____

Monday _____
                                    Date

Time	
5 AM	
6 AM	
7 AM	
8 AM	
9 AM	
10 AM	
11 AM	
12 PM	
1 PM	
2 PM	
3 PM	
4 PM	
5 PM	
6 PM	
7 PM	
8 PM	
9 PM	

Top 3 Goals I'm Setting for Myself Today:
_____
_____
_____

Words & Affirmations I'm Empowering Myself With Today:
_____
_____
_____

Ways I'm Motivating Myself Today:
_____
_____
_____

Ways I'm Bringing Joy into My Day Today:
_____
_____
_____

Tuesday _____
Date

Time	
5 AM	
6 AM	
7 AM	
8 AM	
9 AM	
10 AM	
11 AM	
12 PM	
1 PM	
2 PM	
3 PM	
4 PM	
5 PM	
6 PM	
7 PM	
8 PM	
9 PM	

Top 3 Goals I'm Setting for Myself Today:
_____
_____
_____

Words & Affirmations I'm Empowering Myself With Today:
_____
_____
_____

Ways I'm Motivating Myself Today:
_____
_____
_____

Ways I'm Bringing Joy into My Day Today:
_____
_____
_____

Wednesday _____
Date

Time	
5 AM	
6 AM	
7 AM	
8 AM	
9 AM	
10 AM	
11 AM	
12 PM	
1 PM	
2 PM	
3 PM	
4 PM	
5 PM	
6 PM	
7 PM	
8 PM	
9 PM	

Top 3 Goals I'm Setting for Myself Today:
_____
_____
_____

Words & Affirmations I'm Empowering Myself With Today:
_____
_____
_____

Ways I'm Motivating Myself Today:
_____
_____
_____

Ways I'm Bringing Joy into My Day Today:
_____
_____
_____

Thursday _____
Date

5 AM	
6 AM	
7 AM	
8 AM	
9 AM	
10 AM	
11 AM	
12 PM	
1 PM	
2 PM	
3 PM	
4 PM	
5 PM	
6 PM	
7 PM	
8 PM	
9 PM	

Top 3 Goals I'm Setting for Myself Today:
_____
_____
_____

Words & Affirmations I'm Empowering Myself With Today:
_____
_____
_____

Ways I'm Motivating Myself Today:
_____
_____
_____

Ways I'm Bringing Joy into My Day Today:
_____
_____
_____

Friday _____
Date

5 AM	
6 AM	
7 AM	
8 AM	
9 AM	
10 AM	
11 AM	
12 PM	
1 PM	
2 PM	
3 PM	
4 PM	
5 PM	
6 PM	
7 PM	
8 PM	
9 PM	

Top 3 Goals I'm Setting for Myself Today:
_____
_____
_____

Words & Affirmations I'm Empowering Myself With Today:
_____
_____
_____

Ways I'm Motivating Myself Today:
_____
_____
_____

Ways I'm Bringing Joy into My Day Today:
_____
_____
_____

Saturday _____
Date

Time	
5 AM	
6 AM	
7 AM	
8 AM	
9 AM	
10 AM	
11 AM	
12 PM	
1 PM	
2 PM	
3 PM	
4 PM	
5 PM	
6 PM	
7 PM	
8 PM	
9 PM	

Top 3 Goals I'm Setting for Myself Today:
_____
_____
_____

Words & Affirmations I'm Empowering Myself With Today:
_____
_____
_____

Ways I'm Motivating Myself Today:
_____
_____
_____

Ways I'm Bringing Joy into My Day Today:
_____
_____
_____

My Week in Review

Accomplishments I'm Most Proud of This Week:
_____
_____
_____

Obstacles & Challenges I Triumphed Over This Week:
_____
_____
_____

Ways I Was Kind To Myself & Others This Week:
_____
_____
_____

What I'm Most Grateful For This Week:
_____
_____
_____

Engage Your Goals!

Week #24

"Success is liking yourself, liking what you do, and liking how you do it."
~ Maya Angelou

Revelations From The Research:

Epton, Currie, & Armitage discovered that goal setting has a significant impact on facilitating behavior change, especially if the goal is difficult and set publicly for accountability.[24]

3 Ps Weekly Action Agenda

Week of _____
Date

Professional:

Actions   Complete By

Personal:

Actions   Complete By

Passions:

Actions   Complete By

Longer Term Actions or Projects:

Commitment Calendar

Sunday _____
Date

Time	
5 AM	
6 AM	
7 AM	
8 AM	
9 AM	
10 AM	
11 AM	
12 PM	
1 PM	
2 PM	
3 PM	
4 PM	
5 PM	
6 PM	
7 PM	
8 PM	
9 PM	

Top 3 Goals I'm Setting for Myself Today:
_____
_____
_____

Words & Affirmations I'm Empowering Myself With Today:
_____
_____
_____

Ways I'm Motivating Myself Today:
_____
_____
_____

Ways I'm Bringing Joy into My Day Today:
_____
_____
_____

Monday _____
Date

Time	
5 AM	
6 AM	
7 AM	
8 AM	
9 AM	
10 AM	
11 AM	
12 PM	
1 PM	
2 PM	
3 PM	
4 PM	
5 PM	
6 PM	
7 PM	
8 PM	
9 PM	

Top 3 Goals I'm Setting for Myself Today:
_____
_____
_____

Words & Affirmations I'm Empowering Myself With Today:
_____
_____
_____

Ways I'm Motivating Myself Today:
_____
_____
_____

Ways I'm Bringing Joy into My Day Today:
_____
_____
_____

Tuesday _____
Date

5 AM
6 AM
7 AM
8 AM
9 AM
10 AM
11 AM
12 PM
1 PM
2 PM
3 PM
4 PM
5 PM
6 PM
7 PM
8 PM
9 PM

Top 3 Goals I'm Setting for Myself Today:
_____
_____
_____

Words & Affirmations I'm Empowering Myself With Today:
_____
_____
_____

Ways I'm Motivating Myself Today:
_____
_____
_____

Ways I'm Bringing Joy into My Day Today:
_____
_____
_____

Wednesday _____
Date

5 AM
6 AM
7 AM
8 AM
9 AM
10 AM
11 AM
12 PM
1 PM
2 PM
3 PM
4 PM
5 PM
6 PM
7 PM
8 PM
9 PM

Top 3 Goals I'm Setting for Myself Today:
_____
_____
_____

Words & Affirmations I'm Empowering Myself With Today:
_____
_____
_____

Ways I'm Motivating Myself Today:
_____
_____
_____

Ways I'm Bringing Joy into My Day Today:
_____
_____
_____

Thursday _____
Date

5 AM	**Top 3 Goals I'm Setting for Myself Today:**
6 AM	
7 AM	
8 AM	
9 AM	**Words & Affirmations I'm Empowering Myself With Today:**
10 AM	
11 AM	
12 PM	
1 PM	**Ways I'm Motivating Myself Today:**
2 PM	
3 PM	
4 PM	
5 PM	**Ways I'm Bringing Joy into My Day Today:**
6 PM	
7 PM	
8 PM	
9 PM	

Friday _____
Date

5 AM	**Top 3 Goals I'm Setting for Myself Today:**
6 AM	
7 AM	
8 AM	
9 AM	**Words & Affirmations I'm Empowering Myself With Today:**
10 AM	
11 AM	
12 PM	
1 PM	**Ways I'm Motivating Myself Today:**
2 PM	
3 PM	
4 PM	
5 PM	**Ways I'm Bringing Joy into My Day Today:**
6 PM	
7 PM	
8 PM	
9 PM	

Saturday _____
Date

Time	
5 AM	
6 AM	
7 AM	
8 AM	
9 AM	
10 AM	
11 AM	
12 PM	
1 PM	
2 PM	
3 PM	
4 PM	
5 PM	
6 PM	
7 PM	
8 PM	
9 PM	

Top 3 Goals I'm Setting for Myself Today:
_____
_____
_____

Words & Affirmations I'm Empowering Myself With Today:
_____
_____
_____

Ways I'm Motivating Myself Today:
_____
_____
_____

Ways I'm Bringing Joy into My Day Today:
_____
_____
_____

My Week in Review

Accomplishments I'm Most Proud of This Week:
_____
_____
_____

Obstacles & Challenges I Triumphed Over This Week:
_____
_____
_____

Ways I Was Kind To Myself & Others This Week:
_____
_____
_____

What I'm Most Grateful For This Week:
_____
_____
_____

Engage Your Goals!

Week #25

"When I dare to be powerful, to use my strength in the service of my vision, then it becomes less and less important whether I am afraid."
~ Audre Lorde

Revelations From The Research:

Rubinstein, Meyer, & Evans discovered that doing more than one task at a time, especially multiple complex tasks, takes a considerable toll on productivity and can lead to mental overload and greater likelihood of errors.[25]

3 Ps Weekly Action Agenda

Week of _____
Date

Professional:

Actions — Complete By

Personal:

Actions — Complete By

Passions:

Actions — Complete By

Longer Term Actions or Projects:

Commitment Calendar

Sunday _____
Date

5 AM
6 AM
7 AM
8 AM
9 AM
10 AM
11 AM
12 PM
1 PM
2 PM
3 PM
4 PM
5 PM
6 PM
7 PM
8 PM
9 PM

Top 3 Goals I'm Setting for Myself Today:
_____
_____
_____

Words & Affirmations I'm Empowering Myself With Today:
_____
_____
_____

Ways I'm Motivating Myself Today:
_____
_____
_____

Ways I'm Bringing Joy into My Day Today:
_____
_____
_____

Monday _____
Date

5 AM
6 AM
7 AM
8 AM
9 AM
10 AM
11 AM
12 PM
1 PM
2 PM
3 PM
4 PM
5 PM
6 PM
7 PM
8 PM
9 PM

Top 3 Goals I'm Setting for Myself Today:
_____
_____
_____

Words & Affirmations I'm Empowering Myself With Today:
_____
_____
_____

Ways I'm Motivating Myself Today:
_____
_____
_____

Ways I'm Bringing Joy into My Day Today:
_____
_____
_____

Tuesday _____ Date

Time	
5 AM	
6 AM	
7 AM	
8 AM	
9 AM	
10 AM	
11 AM	
12 PM	
1 PM	
2 PM	
3 PM	
4 PM	
5 PM	
6 PM	
7 PM	
8 PM	
9 PM	

Top 3 Goals I'm Setting for Myself Today:
_____
_____
_____

Words & Affirmations I'm Empowering Myself With Today:
_____
_____

Ways I'm Motivating Myself Today:
_____
_____

Ways I'm Bringing Joy into My Day Today:
_____
_____
_____

Wednesday _____ Date

5 AM	
6 AM	
7 AM	
8 AM	
9 AM	
10 AM	
11 AM	
12 PM	
1 PM	
2 PM	
3 PM	
4 PM	
5 PM	
6 PM	
7 PM	
8 PM	
9 PM	

Top 3 Goals I'm Setting for Myself Today:
_____
_____
_____

Words & Affirmations I'm Empowering Myself With Today:
_____
_____

Ways I'm Motivating Myself Today:
_____
_____

Ways I'm Bringing Joy into My Day Today:
_____
_____
_____

Thursday _____
Date

Time	
5 AM	
6 AM	
7 AM	
8 AM	
9 AM	
10 AM	
11 AM	
12 PM	
1 PM	
2 PM	
3 PM	
4 PM	
5 PM	
6 PM	
7 PM	
8 PM	
9 PM	

Top 3 Goals I'm Setting for Myself Today:
_____
_____
_____

Words & Affirmations I'm Empowering Myself With Today:
_____
_____
_____

Ways I'm Motivating Myself Today:
_____
_____
_____

Ways I'm Bringing Joy into My Day Today:
_____
_____
_____

Friday _____
Date

Time	
5 AM	
6 AM	
7 AM	
8 AM	
9 AM	
10 AM	
11 AM	
12 PM	
1 PM	
2 PM	
3 PM	
4 PM	
5 PM	
6 PM	
7 PM	
8 PM	
9 PM	

Top 3 Goals I'm Setting for Myself Today:
_____
_____
_____

Words & Affirmations I'm Empowering Myself With Today:
_____
_____
_____

Ways I'm Motivating Myself Today:
_____
_____
_____

Ways I'm Bringing Joy into My Day Today:
_____
_____
_____

Saturday _____
Date

Time	
5 AM	
6 AM	
7 AM	
8 AM	
9 AM	
10 AM	
11 AM	
12 PM	
1 PM	
2 PM	
3 PM	
4 PM	
5 PM	
6 PM	
7 PM	
8 PM	
9 PM	

Top 3 Goals I'm Setting for Myself Today:
_____
_____
_____

Words & Affirmations I'm Empowering Myself With Today:
_____
_____
_____

Ways I'm Motivating Myself Today:
_____
_____
_____

Ways I'm Bringing Joy into My Day Today:
_____
_____
_____

My Week in Review

Accomplishments I'm Most Proud of This Week:
_____
_____
_____
_____

Obstacles & Challenges I Triumphed Over This Week:
_____
_____
_____
_____

Ways I Was Kind To Myself & Others This Week:
_____
_____
_____

What I'm Most Grateful For This Week:
_____
_____
_____

Engage Your Goals!

Week #26

"There is no traffic jam along the extra mile."
~ Roger Staubach

Revelations From The Research:

Yukl & Latham led a 10-week workplace study and found that employees who set difficult goals achieved higher performance and those who understood the reason why the goals were necessary were the most successful in tackling them as it enhanced their sense of purpose.[26]

3 Ps Weekly Action Agenda

Week of _____
                        Date

Professional:

Actions	Complete By

Personal:

Actions	Complete By

Passions:

Actions	Complete By

Longer Term Actions or Projects:

Commitment Calendar

Sunday _____
Date

Time	
5 AM	
6 AM	
7 AM	
8 AM	
9 AM	
10 AM	
11 AM	
12 PM	
1 PM	
2 PM	
3 PM	
4 PM	
5 PM	
6 PM	
7 PM	
8 PM	
9 PM	

Top 3 Goals I'm Setting for Myself Today:
_____
_____
_____

Words & Affirmations I'm Empowering Myself With Today:
_____
_____
_____

Ways I'm Motivating Myself Today:
_____
_____
_____

Ways I'm Bringing Joy into My Day Today:
_____
_____
_____

Monday _____
Date

Time	
5 AM	
6 AM	
7 AM	
8 AM	
9 AM	
10 AM	
11 AM	
12 PM	
1 PM	
2 PM	
3 PM	
4 PM	
5 PM	
6 PM	
7 PM	
8 PM	
9 PM	

Top 3 Goals I'm Setting for Myself Today:
_____
_____
_____

Words & Affirmations I'm Empowering Myself With Today:
_____
_____
_____

Ways I'm Motivating Myself Today:
_____
_____
_____

Ways I'm Bringing Joy into My Day Today:
_____
_____
_____

Tuesday _____
Date

Time	
5 AM	
6 AM	
7 AM	
8 AM	
9 AM	
10 AM	
11 AM	
12 PM	
1 PM	
2 PM	
3 PM	
4 PM	
5 PM	
6 PM	
7 PM	
8 PM	
9 PM	

Top 3 Goals I'm Setting for Myself Today:
_____
_____
_____

Words & Affirmations I'm Empowering Myself With Today:
_____
_____
_____

Ways I'm Motivating Myself Today:
_____
_____
_____

Ways I'm Bringing Joy into My Day Today:
_____
_____
_____

Wednesday _____
Date

Time	
5 AM	
6 AM	
7 AM	
8 AM	
9 AM	
10 AM	
11 AM	
12 PM	
1 PM	
2 PM	
3 PM	
4 PM	
5 PM	
6 PM	
7 PM	
8 PM	
9 PM	

Top 3 Goals I'm Setting for Myself Today:
_____
_____
_____

Words & Affirmations I'm Empowering Myself With Today:
_____
_____
_____

Ways I'm Motivating Myself Today:
_____
_____
_____

Ways I'm Bringing Joy into My Day Today:
_____
_____
_____

Thursday _____
Date

Time	
5 AM	
6 AM	
7 AM	
8 AM	
9 AM	
10 AM	
11 AM	
12 PM	
1 PM	
2 PM	
3 PM	
4 PM	
5 PM	
6 PM	
7 PM	
8 PM	
9 PM	

Top 3 Goals I'm Setting for Myself Today:
_____
_____
_____

Words & Affirmations I'm Empowering Myself With Today:
_____
_____
_____

Ways I'm Motivating Myself Today:
_____
_____
_____

Ways I'm Bringing Joy into My Day Today:
_____
_____
_____

Friday _____
Date

Time	
5 AM	
6 AM	
7 AM	
8 AM	
9 AM	
10 AM	
11 AM	
12 PM	
1 PM	
2 PM	
3 PM	
4 PM	
5 PM	
6 PM	
7 PM	
8 PM	
9 PM	

Top 3 Goals I'm Setting for Myself Today:
_____
_____
_____

Words & Affirmations I'm Empowering Myself With Today:
_____
_____
_____

Ways I'm Motivating Myself Today:
_____
_____
_____

Ways I'm Bringing Joy into My Day Today:
_____
_____
_____

Saturday _____
_____Date_____

5 AM	
6 AM	
7 AM	
8 AM	
9 AM	
10 AM	
11 AM	
12 PM	
1 PM	
2 PM	
3 PM	
4 PM	
5 PM	
6 PM	
7 PM	
8 PM	
9 PM	

Top 3 Goals I'm Setting for Myself Today:
_____
_____
_____

Words & Affirmations I'm Empowering Myself With Today:
_____
_____
_____

Ways I'm Motivating Myself Today:
_____
_____
_____

Ways I'm Bringing Joy into My Day Today:
_____
_____
_____

My Week in Review

Accomplishments I'm Most Proud of This Week:
_____
_____
_____

Obstacles & Challenges I Triumphed Over This Week:
_____
_____
_____

Ways I Was Kind To Myself & Others This Week:
_____
_____
_____

What I'm Most Grateful For This Week:
_____
_____
_____

Engage Your Goals!

Week #27

"Develop success from failures. Discouragement and failure are two of the surest stepping stones to success."
~ Dale Carnegie

Revelations From The Research:

Travers, Morisano, & Locke led a study of a 6-month personal growth goal-setting program for college students. They found that setting growth goals facilitated improved stress management, time management, self-control, self-confidence, academic performance, and work-life balance both during the program and after the program ended.[27]

3 Ps Weekly Action Agenda

Week of _____
                                Date

Professional: **Personal:**   **Passions:**

Actions   Complete By   Actions   Complete By   Actions   Complete By

Longer Term Actions or Projects:

Commitment Calendar

Sunday _____

Date

5 AM
6 AM
7 AM
8 AM
9 AM
10 AM
11 AM
12 PM
1 PM
2 PM
3 PM
4 PM
5 PM
6 PM
7 PM
8 PM
9 PM

Top 3 Goals I'm Setting for Myself Today:
_____
_____
_____

Words & Affirmations I'm Empowering Myself With Today:
_____
_____
_____

Ways I'm Motivating Myself Today:
_____
_____
_____

Ways I'm Bringing Joy into My Day Today:
_____
_____
_____

Monday _____

Date

5 AM
6 AM
7 AM
8 AM
9 AM
10 AM
11 AM
12 PM
1 PM
2 PM
3 PM
4 PM
5 PM
6 PM
7 PM
8 PM
9 PM

Top 3 Goals I'm Setting for Myself Today:
_____
_____
_____

Words & Affirmations I'm Empowering Myself With Today:
_____
_____
_____

Ways I'm Motivating Myself Today:
_____
_____
_____

Ways I'm Bringing Joy into My Day Today:
_____
_____
_____

Tuesday _____
                                         Date

Time	
5 AM	
6 AM	
7 AM	
8 AM	
9 AM	
10 AM	
11 AM	
12 PM	
1 PM	
2 PM	
3 PM	
4 PM	
5 PM	
6 PM	
7 PM	
8 PM	
9 PM	

Top 3 Goals I'm Setting for Myself Today:
_____
_____
_____

Words & Affirmations I'm Empowering Myself With Today:
_____
_____
_____

Ways I'm Motivating Myself Today:
_____
_____
_____

Ways I'm Bringing Joy into My Day Today:
_____
_____
_____

Wednesday _____
                                         Date

Time	
5 AM	
6 AM	
7 AM	
8 AM	
9 AM	
10 AM	
11 AM	
12 PM	
1 PM	
2 PM	
3 PM	
4 PM	
5 PM	
6 PM	
7 PM	
8 PM	
9 PM	

Top 3 Goals I'm Setting for Myself Today:
_____
_____
_____

Words & Affirmations I'm Empowering Myself With Today:
_____
_____
_____

Ways I'm Motivating Myself Today:
_____
_____
_____

Ways I'm Bringing Joy into My Day Today:
_____
_____
_____

Thursday _____

Date

Time	
5 AM	
6 AM	
7 AM	
8 AM	
9 AM	
10 AM	
11 AM	
12 PM	
1 PM	
2 PM	
3 PM	
4 PM	
5 PM	
6 PM	
7 PM	
8 PM	
9 PM	

Top 3 Goals I'm Setting for Myself Today:
_____
_____
_____

Words & Affirmations I'm Empowering Myself With Today:
_____
_____
_____

Ways I'm Motivating Myself Today:
_____
_____
_____

Ways I'm Bringing Joy into My Day Today:
_____
_____
_____

Friday _____

Date

Time	
5 AM	
6 AM	
7 AM	
8 AM	
9 AM	
10 AM	
11 AM	
12 PM	
1 PM	
2 PM	
3 PM	
4 PM	
5 PM	
6 PM	
7 PM	
8 PM	
9 PM	

Top 3 Goals I'm Setting for Myself Today:
_____
_____
_____

Words & Affirmations I'm Empowering Myself With Today:
_____
_____
_____

Ways I'm Motivating Myself Today:
_____
_____
_____

Ways I'm Bringing Joy into My Day Today:
_____
_____
_____

Saturday _____
                                          Date

5 AM	Top 3 Goals I'm Setting for Myself Today:
6 AM	_____
7 AM	_____
8 AM	_____
9 AM	Words & Affirmations I'm Empowering Myself With Today:
10 AM	_____
11 AM	_____
12 PM	_____
1 PM	Ways I'm Motivating Myself Today:
2 PM	_____
3 PM	_____
4 PM	_____
5 PM	Ways I'm Bringing Joy into My Day Today:
6 PM	_____
7 PM	_____
8 PM	_____
9 PM	

My Week in Review

Accomplishments I'm Most Proud of This Week:
_____
_____
_____

Obstacles & Challenges I Triumphed Over This Week:
_____
_____
_____

Ways I Was Kind To Myself & Others This Week:
_____
_____
_____

What I'm Most Grateful For This Week:
_____
_____
_____

Engage Your Goals!

Week #28

*"Progress will come in fits and starts.
It's not always a straight line.
It's not always a smooth path."
~ Barack Obama*

Revelations From The Research:

Ariga & Lleras revealed that when working on long tasks, those who take brief breaks during their work experience significantly better focus and memory.[28]

3 Ps Weekly Action Agenda

Week of _____
Date

Professional:

Actions   Complete By

Personal:

Actions   Complete By

Passions:

Actions   Complete By

Longer Term Actions or Projects:

Commitment Calendar

Sunday _____

Date

5 AM	Top 3 Goals I'm Setting for Myself Today:
6 AM	_____
7 AM	_____
8 AM	_____
9 AM	Words & Affirmations I'm Empowering Myself With Today:
10 AM	_____
11 AM	_____
12 PM	_____
1 PM	Ways I'm Motivating Myself Today:
2 PM	_____
3 PM	_____
4 PM	_____
5 PM	Ways I'm Bringing Joy into My Day Today:
6 PM	_____
7 PM	_____
8 PM	_____
9 PM	

Monday _____

Date

5 AM	Top 3 Goals I'm Setting for Myself Today:
6 AM	_____
7 AM	_____
8 AM	_____
9 AM	Words & Affirmations I'm Empowering Myself With Today:
10 AM	_____
11 AM	_____
12 PM	_____
1 PM	Ways I'm Motivating Myself Today:
2 PM	_____
3 PM	_____
4 PM	_____
5 PM	Ways I'm Bringing Joy into My Day Today:
6 PM	_____
7 PM	_____
8 PM	_____
9 PM	

Tuesday _____
                                    Date

Time	
5 AM	
6 AM	
7 AM	
8 AM	
9 AM	
10 AM	
11 AM	
12 PM	
1 PM	
2 PM	
3 PM	
4 PM	
5 PM	
6 PM	
7 PM	
8 PM	
9 PM	

Top 3 Goals I'm Setting for Myself Today:
_____
_____
_____

Words & Affirmations I'm Empowering Myself With Today:
_____
_____

Ways I'm Motivating Myself Today:
_____
_____

Ways I'm Bringing Joy into My Day Today:
_____
_____
_____

Wednesday _____
                                    Date

Time	
5 AM	
6 AM	
7 AM	
8 AM	
9 AM	
10 AM	
11 AM	
12 PM	
1 PM	
2 PM	
3 PM	
4 PM	
5 PM	
6 PM	
7 PM	
8 PM	
9 PM	

Top 3 Goals I'm Setting for Myself Today:
_____
_____
_____

Words & Affirmations I'm Empowering Myself With Today:
_____
_____

Ways I'm Motivating Myself Today:
_____
_____

Ways I'm Bringing Joy into My Day Today:
_____
_____
_____

Thursday _____
Date

5 AM	
6 AM	**Top 3 Goals I'm Setting for Myself Today:**
7 AM	_____
8 AM	_____
9 AM	_____
10 AM	**Words & Affirmations I'm Empowering Myself With Today:**
11 AM	_____
12 PM	_____
1 PM	**Ways I'm Motivating Myself Today:**
2 PM	_____
3 PM	_____
4 PM	_____
5 PM	**Ways I'm Bringing Joy into My Day Today:**
6 PM	_____
7 PM	_____
8 PM	_____
9 PM	

Friday _____
Date

5 AM	
6 AM	**Top 3 Goals I'm Setting for Myself Today:**
7 AM	_____
8 AM	_____
9 AM	_____
10 AM	**Words & Affirmations I'm Empowering Myself With Today:**
11 AM	_____
12 PM	_____
1 PM	**Ways I'm Motivating Myself Today:**
2 PM	_____
3 PM	_____
4 PM	_____
5 PM	**Ways I'm Bringing Joy into My Day Today:**
6 PM	_____
7 PM	_____
8 PM	_____
9 PM	

Saturday _____
Date

Time
5 AM
6 AM
7 AM
8 AM
9 AM
10 AM
11 AM
12 PM
1 PM
2 PM
3 PM
4 PM
5 PM
6 PM
7 PM
8 PM
9 PM

Top 3 Goals I'm Setting for Myself Today:
_____
_____
_____

Words & Affirmations I'm Empowering Myself With Today:
_____
_____

Ways I'm Motivating Myself Today:
_____
_____

Ways I'm Bringing Joy into My Day Today:
_____
_____

My Week in Review

Accomplishments I'm Most Proud of This Week:
_____
_____
_____

Obstacles & Challenges I Triumphed Over This Week:
_____
_____
_____

Ways I Was Kind To Myself & Others This Week:
_____
_____
_____

What I'm Most Grateful For This Week:
_____
_____
_____

Engage Your Goals!

Week #29

"If you don't get out of the box you've been raised in, you won't understand how much bigger the world is."
~ Angelina Jolie

Revelations From The Research:

Moeller, Theiler, & Wu conducted a 5-year experimental study with high school students and found that goal setting has a significantly positive impact on students' academic achievement.[29]

3 Ps Weekly Action Agenda

Week of _____
Date

Professional:

Actions   Complete By

Personal:

Actions   Complete By

Passions:

Actions   Complete By

Longer Term Actions or Projects:

Commitment Calendar

Sunday _____
                                            Date

Time	
5 AM	
6 AM	
7 AM	
8 AM	
9 AM	
10 AM	
11 AM	
12 PM	
1 PM	
2 PM	
3 PM	
4 PM	
5 PM	
6 PM	
7 PM	
8 PM	
9 PM	

Top 3 Goals I'm Setting for Myself Today:
_____
_____
_____

Words & Affirmations I'm Empowering Myself With Today:
_____
_____
_____

Ways I'm Motivating Myself Today:
_____
_____
_____

Ways I'm Bringing Joy into My Day Today:
_____
_____
_____

Monday _____
                                            Date

Time	
5 AM	
6 AM	
7 AM	
8 AM	
9 AM	
10 AM	
11 AM	
12 PM	
1 PM	
2 PM	
3 PM	
4 PM	
5 PM	
6 PM	
7 PM	
8 PM	
9 PM	

Top 3 Goals I'm Setting for Myself Today:
_____
_____
_____

Words & Affirmations I'm Empowering Myself With Today:
_____
_____
_____

Ways I'm Motivating Myself Today:
_____
_____
_____

Ways I'm Bringing Joy into My Day Today:
_____
_____
_____

Tuesday _____
Date

Time	
5 AM	
6 AM	
7 AM	
8 AM	
9 AM	
10 AM	
11 AM	
12 PM	
1 PM	
2 PM	
3 PM	
4 PM	
5 PM	
6 PM	
7 PM	
8 PM	
9 PM	

Top 3 Goals I'm Setting for Myself Today:
_____
_____
_____

Words & Affirmations I'm Empowering Myself With Today:
_____
_____
_____

Ways I'm Motivating Myself Today:
_____
_____
_____

Ways I'm Bringing Joy into My Day Today:
_____
_____
_____

Wednesday _____
Date

Time	
5 AM	
6 AM	
7 AM	
8 AM	
9 AM	
10 AM	
11 AM	
12 PM	
1 PM	
2 PM	
3 PM	
4 PM	
5 PM	
6 PM	
7 PM	
8 PM	
9 PM	

Top 3 Goals I'm Setting for Myself Today:
_____
_____
_____

Words & Affirmations I'm Empowering Myself With Today:
_____
_____
_____

Ways I'm Motivating Myself Today:
_____
_____
_____

Ways I'm Bringing Joy into My Day Today:
_____
_____
_____

Thursday _____

Date

Time	
5 AM	
6 AM	
7 AM	
8 AM	
9 AM	
10 AM	
11 AM	
12 PM	
1 PM	
2 PM	
3 PM	
4 PM	
5 PM	
6 PM	
7 PM	
8 PM	
9 PM	

Top 3 Goals I'm Setting for Myself Today:
_____
_____
_____

Words & Affirmations I'm Empowering Myself With Today:
_____
_____
_____

Ways I'm Motivating Myself Today:
_____
_____
_____

Ways I'm Bringing Joy into My Day Today:
_____
_____
_____

Friday _____

Date

Time	
5 AM	
6 AM	
7 AM	
8 AM	
9 AM	
10 AM	
11 AM	
12 PM	
1 PM	
2 PM	
3 PM	
4 PM	
5 PM	
6 PM	
7 PM	
8 PM	
9 PM	

Top 3 Goals I'm Setting for Myself Today:
_____
_____
_____

Words & Affirmations I'm Empowering Myself With Today:
_____
_____
_____

Ways I'm Motivating Myself Today:
_____
_____
_____

Ways I'm Bringing Joy into My Day Today:
_____
_____
_____

Saturday _____
Date

Time	
5 AM	
6 AM	
7 AM	
8 AM	

Top 3 Goals I'm Setting for Myself Today:
_____
_____
_____

Time	
9 AM	
10 AM	
11 AM	
12 PM	

Words & Affirmations I'm Empowering Myself With Today:
_____
_____
_____

Time	
1 PM	
2 PM	
3 PM	
4 PM	

Ways I'm Motivating Myself Today:
_____
_____
_____

Time	
5 PM	
6 PM	
7 PM	
8 PM	
9 PM	

Ways I'm Bringing Joy into My Day Today:
_____
_____
_____

My Week in Review

Accomplishments I'm Most Proud of This Week:
_____
_____
_____

Obstacles & Challenges I Triumphed Over This Week:
_____
_____
_____

Ways I Was Kind To Myself & Others This Week:
_____
_____
_____

What I'm Most Grateful For This Week:
_____
_____
_____

Engage Your Goals!

Week #30

"Don't look at your feet to see if you are doing it right. Just dance."
~ Anne Lamott

Revelations From The Research:

Schippers, Morisano, Locke, Scheepers, Latham, & Jong had college students participate in a personal goal-setting intervention and uncovered that those who set personal goals for themselves showed a 22% increase in academic performance. They also discovered that it didn't matter if students established academic or non-academic goals; it was the overall process of writing about their goals and outlining their specific strategies for goal attainment that led to an increase in their academic performance.[30]

3 Ps Weekly Action Agenda

Week of _____
Date

Professional:

Actions	Complete By

Personal:

Actions	Complete By

Passions:

Actions	Complete By

Longer Term Actions or Projects:

Commitment Calendar

Sunday _____
Date

Time	
5 AM	
6 AM	
7 AM	
8 AM	
9 AM	
10 AM	
11 AM	
12 PM	
1 PM	
2 PM	
3 PM	
4 PM	
5 PM	
6 PM	
7 PM	
8 PM	
9 PM	

Top 3 Goals I'm Setting for Myself Today:
_____
_____
_____

Words & Affirmations I'm Empowering Myself With Today:
_____
_____
_____

Ways I'm Motivating Myself Today:
_____
_____
_____

Ways I'm Bringing Joy into My Day Today:
_____
_____
_____

Monday _____
Date

Time	
5 AM	
6 AM	
7 AM	
8 AM	
9 AM	
10 AM	
11 AM	
12 PM	
1 PM	
2 PM	
3 PM	
4 PM	
5 PM	
6 PM	
7 PM	
8 PM	
9 PM	

Top 3 Goals I'm Setting for Myself Today:
_____
_____
_____

Words & Affirmations I'm Empowering Myself With Today:
_____
_____
_____

Ways I'm Motivating Myself Today:
_____
_____
_____

Ways I'm Bringing Joy into My Day Today:
_____
_____
_____

Tuesday _____
Date

5 AM
6 AM
7 AM
8 AM
9 AM
10 AM
11 AM
12 PM
1 PM
2 PM
3 PM
4 PM
5 PM
6 PM
7 PM
8 PM
9 PM

Top 3 Goals I'm Setting for Myself Today:
_____
_____
_____

Words & Affirmations I'm Empowering Myself With Today:
_____
_____
_____

Ways I'm Motivating Myself Today:
_____
_____
_____

Ways I'm Bringing Joy into My Day Today:
_____
_____
_____

Wednesday _____
Date

5 AM
6 AM
7 AM
8 AM
9 AM
10 AM
11 AM
12 PM
1 PM
2 PM
3 PM
4 PM
5 PM
6 PM
7 PM
8 PM
9 PM

Top 3 Goals I'm Setting for Myself Today:
_____
_____
_____

Words & Affirmations I'm Empowering Myself With Today:
_____
_____
_____

Ways I'm Motivating Myself Today:
_____
_____
_____

Ways I'm Bringing Joy into My Day Today:
_____
_____
_____

Thursday _____

Date

5 AM	Top 3 Goals I'm Setting for Myself Today:
6 AM	_____
7 AM	_____
8 AM	_____
9 AM	Words & Affirmations I'm Empowering Myself With Today:
10 AM	_____
11 AM	_____
12 PM	_____
1 PM	Ways I'm Motivating Myself Today:
2 PM	_____
3 PM	_____
4 PM	_____
5 PM	Ways I'm Bringing Joy into My Day Today:
6 PM	_____
7 PM	_____
8 PM	_____
9 PM	

Friday _____

Date

5 AM	Top 3 Goals I'm Setting for Myself Today:
6 AM	_____
7 AM	_____
8 AM	_____
9 AM	Words & Affirmations I'm Empowering Myself With Today:
10 AM	_____
11 AM	_____
12 PM	_____
1 PM	Ways I'm Motivating Myself Today:
2 PM	_____
3 PM	_____
4 PM	_____
5 PM	Ways I'm Bringing Joy into My Day Today:
6 PM	_____
7 PM	_____
8 PM	_____
9 PM	

Saturday _____
Date

Time	
5 AM	
6 AM	
7 AM	
8 AM	
9 AM	
10 AM	
11 AM	
12 PM	
1 PM	
2 PM	
3 PM	
4 PM	
5 PM	
6 PM	
7 PM	
8 PM	
9 PM	

Top 3 Goals I'm Setting for Myself Today:
_____
_____
_____

Words & Affirmations I'm Empowering Myself With Today:
_____
_____
_____

Ways I'm Motivating Myself Today:
_____
_____
_____

Ways I'm Bringing Joy into My Day Today:
_____
_____
_____

My Week in Review

Accomplishments I'm Most Proud of This Week:
_____
_____
_____

Obstacles & Challenges I Triumphed Over This Week:
_____
_____
_____

Ways I Was Kind To Myself & Others This Week:
_____
_____
_____

What I'm Most Grateful For This Week:
_____
_____
_____

Engage Your Goals!

Week #31

"When you're through changing, you're through."
~ Martha Stewart

Revelations From The Research:

Aeon, Faber, & Panaccio discovered that engaging in time management techniques drives positive job performance, academic achievement, overall wellbeing, and life satisfaction, as well as minimizes stress.[31]

3 Ps Weekly Action Agenda

Week of _____

Date

Professional:

Actions	Complete By

Personal:

Actions	Complete By

Passions:

Actions	Complete By

Longer Term Actions or Projects:

Commitment Calendar

Sunday _____
                                                                                                 Date

- 5 AM
- 6 AM
- 7 AM
- 8 AM
- 9 AM
- 10 AM
- 11 AM
- 12 PM
- 1 PM
- 2 PM
- 3 PM
- 4 PM
- 5 PM
- 6 PM
- 7 PM
- 8 PM
- 9 PM

Top 3 Goals I'm Setting for Myself Today:
_____
_____
_____

Words & Affirmations I'm Empowering Myself With Today:
_____
_____
_____

Ways I'm Motivating Myself Today:
_____
_____
_____

Ways I'm Bringing Joy into My Day Today:
_____
_____
_____

Monday _____
                                                                                                 Date

- 5 AM
- 6 AM
- 7 AM
- 8 AM
- 9 AM
- 10 AM
- 11 AM
- 12 PM
- 1 PM
- 2 PM
- 3 PM
- 4 PM
- 5 PM
- 6 PM
- 7 PM
- 8 PM
- 9 PM

Top 3 Goals I'm Setting for Myself Today:
_____
_____
_____

Words & Affirmations I'm Empowering Myself With Today:
_____
_____
_____

Ways I'm Motivating Myself Today:
_____
_____
_____

Ways I'm Bringing Joy into My Day Today:
_____
_____
_____

Tuesday _____
Date

5 AM
6 AM
7 AM
8 AM
9 AM
10 AM
11 AM
12 PM
1 PM
2 PM
3 PM
4 PM
5 PM
6 PM
7 PM
8 PM
9 PM

Top 3 Goals I'm Setting for Myself Today:
_____
_____
_____

Words & Affirmations I'm Empowering Myself With Today:
_____
_____
_____

Ways I'm Motivating Myself Today:
_____
_____
_____

Ways I'm Bringing Joy into My Day Today:
_____
_____
_____

Wednesday _____
Date

5 AM
6 AM
7 AM
8 AM
9 AM
10 AM
11 AM
12 PM
1 PM
2 PM
3 PM
4 PM
5 PM
6 PM
7 PM
8 PM
9 PM

Top 3 Goals I'm Setting for Myself Today:
_____
_____
_____

Words & Affirmations I'm Empowering Myself With Today:
_____
_____
_____

Ways I'm Motivating Myself Today:
_____
_____
_____

Ways I'm Bringing Joy into My Day Today:
_____
_____
_____

Thursday _____
Date

5 AM	
6 AM	
7 AM	
8 AM	
9 AM	
10 AM	
11 AM	
12 PM	
1 PM	
2 PM	
3 PM	
4 PM	
5 PM	
6 PM	
7 PM	
8 PM	
9 PM	

Top 3 Goals I'm Setting for Myself Today:
_____
_____
_____

Words & Affirmations I'm Empowering Myself With Today:
_____
_____
_____

Ways I'm Motivating Myself Today:
_____
_____
_____

Ways I'm Bringing Joy into My Day Today:
_____
_____
_____

Friday _____
Date

5 AM	
6 AM	
7 AM	
8 AM	
9 AM	
10 AM	
11 AM	
12 PM	
1 PM	
2 PM	
3 PM	
4 PM	
5 PM	
6 PM	
7 PM	
8 PM	
9 PM	

Top 3 Goals I'm Setting for Myself Today:
_____
_____
_____

Words & Affirmations I'm Empowering Myself With Today:
_____
_____
_____

Ways I'm Motivating Myself Today:
_____
_____
_____

Ways I'm Bringing Joy into My Day Today:
_____
_____
_____

Saturday _____
Date

- 5 AM
- 6 AM
- 7 AM
- 8 AM
- 9 AM
- 10 AM
- 11 AM
- 12 PM
- 1 PM
- 2 PM
- 3 PM
- 4 PM
- 5 PM
- 6 PM
- 7 PM
- 8 PM
- 9 PM

Top 3 Goals I'm Setting for Myself Today:
_____
_____
_____

Words & Affirmations I'm Empowering Myself With Today:
_____
_____

Ways I'm Motivating Myself Today:
_____
_____
_____

Ways I'm Bringing Joy into My Day Today:
_____
_____
_____

My Week in Review

Accomplishments I'm Most Proud of This Week:
_____
_____
_____

Obstacles & Challenges I Triumphed Over This Week:
_____
_____
_____

Ways I Was Kind To Myself & Others This Week:
_____
_____
_____

What I'm Most Grateful For This Week:
_____
_____
_____

Engage Your Goals!

Week #32

"It's not the absence of fear, it's overcoming it. Sometimes you've got to blast through and have faith."
~ Emma Watson

Revelations From The Research:

van der Hoek, Groeneveld, & Kuipers conducted a study of adults in the workplace and discovered that establishing clear team goals considerably enhances team effectiveness and efficiency.[32]

3 Ps Weekly Action Agenda

Week of _____
                          Date

Professional:		**Personal:**		**Passions:**	
Actions	Complete By	Actions	Complete By	Actions	Complete By

Longer Term Actions or Projects:

Commitment Calendar

Sunday _____
Date

5 AM	
6 AM	
7 AM	
8 AM	
9 AM	
10 AM	
11 AM	
12 PM	
1 PM	
2 PM	
3 PM	
4 PM	
5 PM	
6 PM	
7 PM	
8 PM	
9 PM	

Top 3 Goals I'm Setting for Myself Today:
_____
_____
_____

Words & Affirmations I'm Empowering Myself With Today:
_____
_____
_____

Ways I'm Motivating Myself Today:
_____
_____
_____

Ways I'm Bringing Joy into My Day Today:
_____
_____
_____

Monday _____
Date

5 AM	
6 AM	
7 AM	
8 AM	
9 AM	
10 AM	
11 AM	
12 PM	
1 PM	
2 PM	
3 PM	
4 PM	
5 PM	
6 PM	
7 PM	
8 PM	
9 PM	

Top 3 Goals I'm Setting for Myself Today:
_____
_____
_____

Words & Affirmations I'm Empowering Myself With Today:
_____
_____
_____

Ways I'm Motivating Myself Today:
_____
_____
_____

Ways I'm Bringing Joy into My Day Today:
_____
_____
_____

Tuesday _____
Date

5 AM	
6 AM	
7 AM	
8 AM	
9 AM	
10 AM	
11 AM	
12 PM	
1 PM	
2 PM	
3 PM	
4 PM	
5 PM	
6 PM	
7 PM	
8 PM	
9 PM	

Top 3 Goals I'm Setting for Myself Today:
_____
_____
_____

Words & Affirmations I'm Empowering Myself With Today:
_____
_____
_____

Ways I'm Motivating Myself Today:
_____
_____
_____

Ways I'm Bringing Joy into My Day Today:
_____
_____
_____

Wednesday _____
Date

5 AM	
6 AM	
7 AM	
8 AM	
9 AM	
10 AM	
11 AM	
12 PM	
1 PM	
2 PM	
3 PM	
4 PM	
5 PM	
6 PM	
7 PM	
8 PM	
9 PM	

Top 3 Goals I'm Setting for Myself Today:
_____
_____
_____

Words & Affirmations I'm Empowering Myself With Today:
_____
_____
_____

Ways I'm Motivating Myself Today:
_____
_____
_____

Ways I'm Bringing Joy into My Day Today:
_____
_____
_____

Thursday _____
                                    Date

Time	
5 AM	
6 AM	
7 AM	
8 AM	
9 AM	
10 AM	
11 AM	
12 PM	
1 PM	
2 PM	
3 PM	
4 PM	
5 PM	
6 PM	
7 PM	
8 PM	
9 PM	

Top 3 Goals I'm Setting for Myself Today:
_____
_____
_____

Words & Affirmations I'm Empowering Myself With Today:
_____
_____
_____

Ways I'm Motivating Myself Today:
_____
_____
_____

Ways I'm Bringing Joy into My Day Today:
_____
_____
_____

Friday _____
                                    Date

Time	
5 AM	
6 AM	
7 AM	
8 AM	
9 AM	
10 AM	
11 AM	
12 PM	
1 PM	
2 PM	
3 PM	
4 PM	
5 PM	
6 PM	
7 PM	
8 PM	
9 PM	

Top 3 Goals I'm Setting for Myself Today:
_____
_____
_____

Words & Affirmations I'm Empowering Myself With Today:
_____
_____
_____

Ways I'm Motivating Myself Today:
_____
_____
_____

Ways I'm Bringing Joy into My Day Today:
_____
_____
_____

Saturday _____
                                   Date

Time	
5 AM	
6 AM	
7 AM	
8 AM	
9 AM	
10 AM	
11 AM	
12 PM	
1 PM	
2 PM	
3 PM	
4 PM	
5 PM	
6 PM	
7 PM	
8 PM	
9 PM	

Top 3 Goals I'm Setting for Myself Today:
_____
_____
_____

Words & Affirmations I'm Empowering Myself With Today:
_____
_____

Ways I'm Motivating Myself Today:
_____
_____

Ways I'm Bringing Joy into My Day Today:
_____
_____

My Week in Review

Accomplishments I'm Most Proud of This Week:
_____
_____
_____

Obstacles & Challenges I Triumphed Over This Week:
_____
_____
_____

Ways I Was Kind To Myself & Others This Week:
_____
_____
_____

What I'm Most Grateful For This Week:
_____
_____
_____

Engage Your Goals!

Week #33

"You must expect great things of yourself before you can do them."
~ Michael Jordan

Revelations From The Research:

Shivetts conducted a 4-week individual goal-setting intervention program with intermediate-level golfers that revealed a significant relationship between goal-setting and driving accuracy performance.[33]

3 Ps Weekly Action Agenda

Week of _____
Date

Professional:

Actions	Complete By

Personal:

Actions	Complete By

Passions:

Actions	Complete By

Longer Term Actions or Projects:

Commitment Calendar

Sunday _____

Date

5 AM
6 AM
7 AM
8 AM
9 AM
10 AM
11 AM
12 PM
1 PM
2 PM
3 PM
4 PM
5 PM
6 PM
7 PM
8 PM
9 PM

Top 3 Goals I'm Setting for Myself Today:
_____
_____
_____

Words & Affirmations I'm Empowering Myself With Today:
_____
_____
_____

Ways I'm Motivating Myself Today:
_____
_____
_____

Ways I'm Bringing Joy into My Day Today:
_____
_____
_____

Monday _____

Date

5 AM
6 AM
7 AM
8 AM
9 AM
10 AM
11 AM
12 PM
1 PM
2 PM
3 PM
4 PM
5 PM
6 PM
7 PM
8 PM
9 PM

Top 3 Goals I'm Setting for Myself Today:
_____
_____
_____

Words & Affirmations I'm Empowering Myself With Today:
_____
_____
_____

Ways I'm Motivating Myself Today:
_____
_____
_____

Ways I'm Bringing Joy into My Day Today:
_____
_____
_____

Tuesday _____
Date

Time	
5 AM	
6 AM	
7 AM	
8 AM	
9 AM	
10 AM	
11 AM	
12 PM	
1 PM	
2 PM	
3 PM	
4 PM	
5 PM	
6 PM	
7 PM	
8 PM	
9 PM	

Top 3 Goals I'm Setting for Myself Today:
_____
_____
_____

Words & Affirmations I'm Empowering Myself With Today:
_____
_____
_____

Ways I'm Motivating Myself Today:
_____
_____
_____

Ways I'm Bringing Joy into My Day Today:
_____
_____
_____

Wednesday _____
Date

Time	
5 AM	
6 AM	
7 AM	
8 AM	
9 AM	
10 AM	
11 AM	
12 PM	
1 PM	
2 PM	
3 PM	
4 PM	
5 PM	
6 PM	
7 PM	
8 PM	
9 PM	

Top 3 Goals I'm Setting for Myself Today:
_____
_____
_____

Words & Affirmations I'm Empowering Myself With Today:
_____
_____
_____

Ways I'm Motivating Myself Today:
_____
_____
_____

Ways I'm Bringing Joy into My Day Today:
_____
_____
_____

Thursday _____
Date

5 AM	
6 AM	
7 AM	
8 AM	
9 AM	
10 AM	
11 AM	
12 PM	
1 PM	
2 PM	
3 PM	
4 PM	
5 PM	
6 PM	
7 PM	
8 PM	
9 PM	

Top 3 Goals I'm Setting for Myself Today:
_____
_____
_____

Words & Affirmations I'm Empowering Myself With Today:
_____
_____
_____

Ways I'm Motivating Myself Today:
_____
_____
_____

Ways I'm Bringing Joy into My Day Today:
_____
_____
_____

Friday _____
Date

5 AM	
6 AM	
7 AM	
8 AM	
9 AM	
10 AM	
11 AM	
12 PM	
1 PM	
2 PM	
3 PM	
4 PM	
5 PM	
6 PM	
7 PM	
8 PM	
9 PM	

Top 3 Goals I'm Setting for Myself Today:
_____
_____
_____

Words & Affirmations I'm Empowering Myself With Today:
_____
_____
_____

Ways I'm Motivating Myself Today:
_____
_____
_____

Ways I'm Bringing Joy into My Day Today:
_____
_____
_____

Saturday _____

Date

Time	
5 AM	
6 AM	
7 AM	
8 AM	
9 AM	
10 AM	
11 AM	
12 PM	
1 PM	
2 PM	
3 PM	
4 PM	
5 PM	
6 PM	
7 PM	
8 PM	
9 PM	

Top 3 Goals I'm Setting for Myself Today:
_____
_____
_____

Words & Affirmations I'm Empowering Myself With Today:
_____
_____

Ways I'm Motivating Myself Today:
_____
_____

Ways I'm Bringing Joy into My Day Today:
_____
_____
_____

My Week in Review

Accomplishments I'm Most Proud of This Week:
_____
_____
_____

Obstacles & Challenges I Triumphed Over This Week:
_____
_____
_____

Ways I Was Kind To Myself & Others This Week:
_____
_____
_____

What I'm Most Grateful For This Week:
_____
_____
_____

Engage Your Goals!

Week #34

*"There is no chance, no destiny, no fate,
that can hinder or control the
firm resolve of a determined soul."
~ Ella Wheeler Wilcox*

Revelations From The Research:

Häfner, Stock, & Oberst performed a study with college students in which they had participants engage in a time management training program. The study revealed that students' feelings of stress decreased and feelings of control over their time increased after training, enhancing students' overall wellbeing.[34]

3 Ps Weekly Action Agenda

Week of _____
            Date

Professional: **Personal:**   **Passions:**

Actions   Complete By   Actions   Complete By   Actions   Complete By

Longer Term Actions or Projects:

Commitment Calendar

Sunday _____
Date

Time	
5 AM	
6 AM	
7 AM	
8 AM	
9 AM	
10 AM	
11 AM	
12 PM	
1 PM	
2 PM	
3 PM	
4 PM	
5 PM	
6 PM	
7 PM	
8 PM	
9 PM	

Top 3 Goals I'm Setting for Myself Today:
_____
_____
_____

Words & Affirmations I'm Empowering Myself With Today:
_____
_____
_____

Ways I'm Motivating Myself Today:
_____
_____
_____

Ways I'm Bringing Joy into My Day Today:
_____
_____
_____

Monday _____
Date

Time	
5 AM	
6 AM	
7 AM	
8 AM	
9 AM	
10 AM	
11 AM	
12 PM	
1 PM	
2 PM	
3 PM	
4 PM	
5 PM	
6 PM	
7 PM	
8 PM	
9 PM	

Top 3 Goals I'm Setting for Myself Today:
_____
_____
_____

Words & Affirmations I'm Empowering Myself With Today:
_____
_____
_____

Ways I'm Motivating Myself Today:
_____
_____
_____

Ways I'm Bringing Joy into My Day Today:
_____
_____
_____

Tuesday _____
Date

Time	
5 AM	
6 AM	
7 AM	
8 AM	
9 AM	
10 AM	
11 AM	
12 PM	
1 PM	
2 PM	
3 PM	
4 PM	
5 PM	
6 PM	
7 PM	
8 PM	
9 PM	

Top 3 Goals I'm Setting for Myself Today:
_____
_____
_____

Words & Affirmations I'm Empowering Myself With Today:
_____
_____
_____

Ways I'm Motivating Myself Today:
_____
_____
_____

Ways I'm Bringing Joy into My Day Today:
_____
_____
_____

Wednesday _____
Date

Time	
5 AM	
6 AM	
7 AM	
8 AM	
9 AM	
10 AM	
11 AM	
12 PM	
1 PM	
2 PM	
3 PM	
4 PM	
5 PM	
6 PM	
7 PM	
8 PM	
9 PM	

Top 3 Goals I'm Setting for Myself Today:
_____
_____
_____

Words & Affirmations I'm Empowering Myself With Today:
_____
_____
_____

Ways I'm Motivating Myself Today:
_____
_____
_____

Ways I'm Bringing Joy into My Day Today:
_____
_____
_____

Thursday _____
Date

Time	
5 AM	
6 AM	
7 AM	
8 AM	
9 AM	
10 AM	
11 AM	
12 PM	
1 PM	
2 PM	
3 PM	
4 PM	
5 PM	
6 PM	
7 PM	
8 PM	
9 PM	

Top 3 Goals I'm Setting for Myself Today:
_____
_____
_____

Words & Affirmations I'm Empowering Myself With Today:
_____
_____
_____

Ways I'm Motivating Myself Today:
_____
_____
_____

Ways I'm Bringing Joy into My Day Today:
_____
_____
_____

Friday _____
Date

Time	
5 AM	
6 AM	
7 AM	
8 AM	
9 AM	
10 AM	
11 AM	
12 PM	
1 PM	
2 PM	
3 PM	
4 PM	
5 PM	
6 PM	
7 PM	
8 PM	
9 PM	

Top 3 Goals I'm Setting for Myself Today:
_____
_____
_____

Words & Affirmations I'm Empowering Myself With Today:
_____
_____
_____

Ways I'm Motivating Myself Today:
_____
_____
_____

Ways I'm Bringing Joy into My Day Today:
_____
_____
_____

Saturday _____
Date

Time	
5 AM	
6 AM	
7 AM	
8 AM	
9 AM	
10 AM	
11 AM	
12 PM	
1 PM	
2 PM	
3 PM	
4 PM	
5 PM	
6 PM	
7 PM	
8 PM	
9 PM	

Top 3 Goals I'm Setting for Myself Today:
_____
_____
_____

Words & Affirmations I'm Empowering Myself With Today:
_____
_____
_____

Ways I'm Motivating Myself Today:
_____
_____
_____

Ways I'm Bringing Joy into My Day Today:
_____
_____
_____

My Week in Review

Accomplishments I'm Most Proud of This Week:
_____
_____
_____
_____

Obstacles & Challenges I Triumphed Over This Week:
_____
_____
_____
_____

Ways I Was Kind To Myself & Others This Week:
_____
_____
_____
_____

What I'm Most Grateful For This Week:
_____
_____
_____
_____

Engage Your Goals!

Week #35

*"You've got to get up every morning with
determination if you're going to
go to bed with satisfaction."*
~ George Lorimer

Revelations From The Research:

Teo & Low discovered that goal setting positively impacts employee effectiveness and organization effectiveness.[35]

3 Ps Weekly Action Agenda

Week of _____
Date

Professional:

Actions	Complete By

Personal:

Actions	Complete By

Passions:

Actions	Complete By

Longer Term Actions or Projects:

Commitment Calendar

Sunday _____

Date _____

5 AM
6 AM
7 AM
8 AM
9 AM
10 AM
11 AM
12 PM
1 PM
2 PM
3 PM
4 PM
5 PM
6 PM
7 PM
8 PM
9 PM

Top 3 Goals I'm Setting for Myself Today:
_____
_____
_____

Words & Affirmations I'm Empowering Myself With Today:
_____
_____
_____

Ways I'm Motivating Myself Today:
_____
_____
_____

Ways I'm Bringing Joy into My Day Today:
_____
_____
_____

Monday _____

Date _____

5 AM
6 AM
7 AM
8 AM
9 AM
10 AM
11 AM
12 PM
1 PM
2 PM
3 PM
4 PM
5 PM
6 PM
7 PM
8 PM
9 PM

Top 3 Goals I'm Setting for Myself Today:
_____
_____
_____

Words & Affirmations I'm Empowering Myself With Today:
_____
_____
_____

Ways I'm Motivating Myself Today:
_____
_____
_____

Ways I'm Bringing Joy into My Day Today:
_____
_____
_____

Tuesday _____
Date

5 AM	**Top 3 Goals I'm Setting for Myself Today:**
6 AM	_____
7 AM	_____
8 AM	_____
9 AM	**Words & Affirmations I'm Empowering Myself With Today:**
10 AM	_____
11 AM	_____
12 PM	_____
1 PM	**Ways I'm Motivating Myself Today:**
2 PM	_____
3 PM	_____
4 PM	_____
5 PM	**Ways I'm Bringing Joy into My Day Today:**
6 PM	_____
7 PM	_____
8 PM	_____
9 PM	

Wednesday _____
Date

5 AM	**Top 3 Goals I'm Setting for Myself Today:**
6 AM	_____
7 AM	_____
8 AM	_____
9 AM	**Words & Affirmations I'm Empowering Myself With Today:**
10 AM	_____
11 AM	_____
12 PM	_____
1 PM	**Ways I'm Motivating Myself Today:**
2 PM	_____
3 PM	_____
4 PM	_____
5 PM	**Ways I'm Bringing Joy into My Day Today:**
6 PM	_____
7 PM	_____
8 PM	_____
9 PM	

Thursday _____
Date

Time	
5 AM	
6 AM	
7 AM	
8 AM	
9 AM	
10 AM	
11 AM	
12 PM	
1 PM	
2 PM	
3 PM	
4 PM	
5 PM	
6 PM	
7 PM	
8 PM	
9 PM	

Top 3 Goals I'm Setting for Myself Today:
_____
_____
_____

Words & Affirmations I'm Empowering Myself With Today:
_____
_____
_____

Ways I'm Motivating Myself Today:
_____
_____
_____

Ways I'm Bringing Joy into My Day Today:
_____
_____
_____

Friday _____
Date

Time	
5 AM	
6 AM	
7 AM	
8 AM	
9 AM	
10 AM	
11 AM	
12 PM	
1 PM	
2 PM	
3 PM	
4 PM	
5 PM	
6 PM	
7 PM	
8 PM	
9 PM	

Top 3 Goals I'm Setting for Myself Today:
_____
_____
_____

Words & Affirmations I'm Empowering Myself With Today:
_____
_____
_____

Ways I'm Motivating Myself Today:
_____
_____
_____

Ways I'm Bringing Joy into My Day Today:
_____
_____
_____

Saturday _____
Date

5 AM	
6 AM	
7 AM	
8 AM	
9 AM	
10 AM	
11 AM	
12 PM	
1 PM	
2 PM	
3 PM	
4 PM	
5 PM	
6 PM	
7 PM	
8 PM	
9 PM	

Top 3 Goals I'm Setting for Myself Today:
_____
_____
_____

Words & Affirmations I'm Empowering Myself With Today:
_____
_____
_____

Ways I'm Motivating Myself Today:
_____
_____
_____

Ways I'm Bringing Joy into My Day Today:
_____
_____
_____

My Week in Review

Accomplishments I'm Most Proud of This Week:
_____
_____
_____

Obstacles & Challenges I Triumphed Over This Week:
_____
_____
_____

Ways I Was Kind To Myself & Others This Week:
_____
_____
_____

What I'm Most Grateful For This Week:
_____
_____
_____

Engage Your Goals!

Week #36

"Success is ... knowing your purpose in life, growing to reach your maximum potential, and sowing seeds that benefit others."
~ John C. Maxwell

Revelations From The Research:

Asmus, Karl, Mohnen, & Reinhart conducted a study with professionals and found that even without financial incentives, goal setting improves worker performance by 12 to 15%.[36]

3 Ps Weekly Action Agenda

Week of _____
Date

Professional:

Actions	Complete By

Personal:

Actions	Complete By

Passions:

Actions	Complete By

Longer Term Actions or Projects:

Commitment Calendar

Sunday _____
Date

Time	
5 AM	
6 AM	
7 AM	
8 AM	
9 AM	
10 AM	
11 AM	
12 PM	
1 PM	
2 PM	
3 PM	
4 PM	
5 PM	
6 PM	
7 PM	
8 PM	
9 PM	

Top 3 Goals I'm Setting for Myself Today:
_____
_____
_____

Words & Affirmations I'm Empowering Myself With Today:
_____
_____
_____

Ways I'm Motivating Myself Today:
_____
_____
_____

Ways I'm Bringing Joy into My Day Today:
_____
_____
_____

Monday _____
Date

Time	
5 AM	
6 AM	
7 AM	
8 AM	
9 AM	
10 AM	
11 AM	
12 PM	
1 PM	
2 PM	
3 PM	
4 PM	
5 PM	
6 PM	
7 PM	
8 PM	
9 PM	

Top 3 Goals I'm Setting for Myself Today:
_____
_____
_____

Words & Affirmations I'm Empowering Myself With Today:
_____
_____
_____

Ways I'm Motivating Myself Today:
_____
_____
_____

Ways I'm Bringing Joy into My Day Today:
_____
_____
_____

Tuesday _____
Date

Time	
5 AM	
6 AM	
7 AM	
8 AM	
9 AM	
10 AM	
11 AM	
12 PM	
1 PM	
2 PM	
3 PM	
4 PM	
5 PM	
6 PM	
7 PM	
8 PM	
9 PM	

Top 3 Goals I'm Setting for Myself Today:
_____
_____
_____

Words & Affirmations I'm Empowering Myself With Today:
_____
_____
_____

Ways I'm Motivating Myself Today:
_____
_____
_____

Ways I'm Bringing Joy into My Day Today:
_____
_____
_____

Wednesday _____
Date

Time	
5 AM	
6 AM	
7 AM	
8 AM	
9 AM	
10 AM	
11 AM	
12 PM	
1 PM	
2 PM	
3 PM	
4 PM	
5 PM	
6 PM	
7 PM	
8 PM	
9 PM	

Top 3 Goals I'm Setting for Myself Today:
_____
_____
_____

Words & Affirmations I'm Empowering Myself With Today:
_____
_____
_____

Ways I'm Motivating Myself Today:
_____
_____
_____

Ways I'm Bringing Joy into My Day Today:
_____
_____
_____

Thursday _____
Date

5 AM	
6 AM	
7 AM	
8 AM	
9 AM	
10 AM	
11 AM	
12 PM	
1 PM	
2 PM	
3 PM	
4 PM	
5 PM	
6 PM	
7 PM	
8 PM	
9 PM	

Top 3 Goals I'm Setting for Myself Today:
_____
_____
_____

Words & Affirmations I'm Empowering Myself With Today:
_____
_____
_____

Ways I'm Motivating Myself Today:
_____
_____
_____

Ways I'm Bringing Joy into My Day Today:
_____
_____
_____

Friday _____
Date

5 AM	
6 AM	
7 AM	
8 AM	
9 AM	
10 AM	
11 AM	
12 PM	
1 PM	
2 PM	
3 PM	
4 PM	
5 PM	
6 PM	
7 PM	
8 PM	
9 PM	

Top 3 Goals I'm Setting for Myself Today:
_____
_____
_____

Words & Affirmations I'm Empowering Myself With Today:
_____
_____
_____

Ways I'm Motivating Myself Today:
_____
_____
_____

Ways I'm Bringing Joy into My Day Today:
_____
_____
_____

Saturday _____
                                              Date

Time	
5 AM	
6 AM	
7 AM	
8 AM	
9 AM	
10 AM	
11 AM	
12 PM	
1 PM	
2 PM	
3 PM	
4 PM	
5 PM	
6 PM	
7 PM	
8 PM	
9 PM	

Top 3 Goals I'm Setting for Myself Today:
_____
_____
_____

Words & Affirmations I'm Empowering Myself With Today:
_____
_____
_____

Ways I'm Motivating Myself Today:
_____
_____
_____

Ways I'm Bringing Joy into My Day Today:
_____
_____
_____

My Week in Review

Accomplishments I'm Most Proud of This Week:
_____
_____
_____
_____

Obstacles & Challenges I Triumphed Over This Week:
_____
_____
_____
_____

Ways I Was Kind To Myself & Others This Week:
_____
_____
_____
_____

What I'm Most Grateful For This Week:
_____
_____
_____
_____

Engage Your Goals!

Week #37

*"Be miserable. Or motivate yourself.
Whatever has to be done,
it's always your choice."*
~Wayne Dyer

Revelations From The Research:

Claessens, van Eerde, Rutte, & Roe reviewed multiple time management research studies and found that engaging in time management behaviors positively impacts job satisfaction, overall health, perceived control of time, and reduces experiences of stress.[37]

3 Ps Weekly Action Agenda

Week of _____
Date

Professional:

Actions	Complete By

Personal:

Actions	Complete By

Passions:

Actions	Complete By

Longer Term Actions or Projects:

Commitment Calendar

Sunday _____
                                            Date

Time	
5 AM	
6 AM	
7 AM	
8 AM	
9 AM	
10 AM	
11 AM	
12 PM	
1 PM	
2 PM	
3 PM	
4 PM	
5 PM	
6 PM	
7 PM	
8 PM	
9 PM	

Top 3 Goals I'm Setting for Myself Today:
_____
_____
_____

Words & Affirmations I'm Empowering Myself With Today:
_____
_____
_____

Ways I'm Motivating Myself Today:
_____
_____
_____

Ways I'm Bringing Joy into My Day Today:
_____
_____
_____

Monday _____
                                            Date

Time	
5 AM	
6 AM	
7 AM	
8 AM	
9 AM	
10 AM	
11 AM	
12 PM	
1 PM	
2 PM	
3 PM	
4 PM	
5 PM	
6 PM	
7 PM	
8 PM	
9 PM	

Top 3 Goals I'm Setting for Myself Today:
_____
_____
_____

Words & Affirmations I'm Empowering Myself With Today:
_____
_____
_____

Ways I'm Motivating Myself Today:
_____
_____
_____

Ways I'm Bringing Joy into My Day Today:
_____
_____
_____

Tuesday _____
                                   Date

Time	
5 AM	
6 AM	
7 AM	
8 AM	
9 AM	
10 AM	
11 AM	
12 PM	
1 PM	
2 PM	
3 PM	
4 PM	
5 PM	
6 PM	
7 PM	
8 PM	
9 PM	

Top 3 Goals I'm Setting for Myself Today:
_____
_____
_____

Words & Affirmations I'm Empowering Myself With Today:
_____
_____
_____

Ways I'm Motivating Myself Today:
_____
_____
_____

Ways I'm Bringing Joy into My Day Today:
_____
_____
_____

Wednesday _____
                                       Date

Time	
5 AM	
6 AM	
7 AM	
8 AM	
9 AM	
10 AM	
11 AM	
12 PM	
1 PM	
2 PM	
3 PM	
4 PM	
5 PM	
6 PM	
7 PM	
8 PM	
9 PM	

Top 3 Goals I'm Setting for Myself Today:
_____
_____
_____

Words & Affirmations I'm Empowering Myself With Today:
_____
_____
_____

Ways I'm Motivating Myself Today:
_____
_____
_____

Ways I'm Bringing Joy into My Day Today:
_____
_____
_____

Thursday _____
Date

Time	
5 AM	
6 AM	
7 AM	
8 AM	
9 AM	
10 AM	
11 AM	
12 PM	
1 PM	
2 PM	
3 PM	
4 PM	
5 PM	
6 PM	
7 PM	
8 PM	
9 PM	

Top 3 Goals I'm Setting for Myself Today:
_____
_____
_____

Words & Affirmations I'm Empowering Myself With Today:
_____
_____
_____

Ways I'm Motivating Myself Today:
_____
_____
_____

Ways I'm Bringing Joy into My Day Today:
_____
_____
_____

Friday _____
Date

Time	
5 AM	
6 AM	
7 AM	
8 AM	
9 AM	
10 AM	
11 AM	
12 PM	
1 PM	
2 PM	
3 PM	
4 PM	
5 PM	
6 PM	
7 PM	
8 PM	
9 PM	

Top 3 Goals I'm Setting for Myself Today:
_____
_____
_____

Words & Affirmations I'm Empowering Myself With Today:
_____
_____
_____

Ways I'm Motivating Myself Today:
_____
_____
_____

Ways I'm Bringing Joy into My Day Today:
_____
_____
_____

3 Ps Weekly Action Agenda

Week of _____
                           Date

Professional:

Actions   Complete By

Personal:

Actions   Complete By

Passions:

Actions   Complete By

Longer Term Actions or Projects:

Commitment Calendar

Sunday _____
                                    Date

5 AM
6 AM
7 AM
8 AM   Top 3 Goals I'm Setting for Myself Today:
9 AM   _____
10 AM _____
11 AM _____
12 PM
       Words & Affirmations I'm Empowering Myself With Today:
1 PM   _____
2 PM   _____
3 PM   _____
4 PM
       Ways I'm Motivating Myself Today:
5 PM   _____
6 PM   _____
7 PM   _____
8 PM
9 PM   Ways I'm Bringing Joy into My Day Today:
       _____
       _____
       _____

Monday _____
                                    Date

5 AM
6 AM
7 AM
8 AM   Top 3 Goals I'm Setting for Myself Today:
9 AM   _____
10 AM _____
11 AM _____
12 PM
       Words & Affirmations I'm Empowering Myself With Today:
1 PM   _____
2 PM   _____
3 PM   _____
4 PM
       Ways I'm Motivating Myself Today:
5 PM   _____
6 PM   _____
7 PM   _____
8 PM
9 PM   Ways I'm Bringing Joy into My Day Today:
       _____
       _____
       _____

Tuesday _____
Date

5 AM
6 AM
7 AM
8 AM
9 AM
10 AM
11 AM
12 PM
1 PM
2 PM
3 PM
4 PM
5 PM
6 PM
7 PM
8 PM
9 PM

Top 3 Goals I'm Setting for Myself Today:
_____
_____
_____

Words & Affirmations I'm Empowering Myself With Today:
_____
_____
_____

Ways I'm Motivating Myself Today:
_____
_____
_____

Ways I'm Bringing Joy into My Day Today:
_____
_____
_____

Wednesday _____
Date

5 AM
6 AM
7 AM
8 AM
9 AM
10 AM
11 AM
12 PM
1 PM
2 PM
3 PM
4 PM
5 PM
6 PM
7 PM
8 PM
9 PM

Top 3 Goals I'm Setting for Myself Today:
_____
_____
_____

Words & Affirmations I'm Empowering Myself With Today:
_____
_____
_____

Ways I'm Motivating Myself Today:
_____
_____
_____

Ways I'm Bringing Joy into My Day Today:
_____
_____
_____

Thursday _____
Date

Time	
5 AM	
6 AM	
7 AM	
8 AM	
9 AM	
10 AM	
11 AM	
12 PM	
1 PM	
2 PM	
3 PM	
4 PM	
5 PM	
6 PM	
7 PM	
8 PM	
9 PM	

Top 3 Goals I'm Setting for Myself Today:
_____
_____
_____

Words & Affirmations I'm Empowering Myself With Today:
_____
_____
_____

Ways I'm Motivating Myself Today:
_____
_____
_____

Ways I'm Bringing Joy into My Day Today:
_____
_____
_____

Friday _____
Date

Time	
5 AM	
6 AM	
7 AM	
8 AM	
9 AM	
10 AM	
11 AM	
12 PM	
1 PM	
2 PM	
3 PM	
4 PM	
5 PM	
6 PM	
7 PM	
8 PM	
9 PM	

Top 3 Goals I'm Setting for Myself Today:
_____
_____
_____

Words & Affirmations I'm Empowering Myself With Today:
_____
_____
_____

Ways I'm Motivating Myself Today:
_____
_____
_____

Ways I'm Bringing Joy into My Day Today:
_____
_____
_____

Saturday _____
                                             Date

Time
5 AM
6 AM
7 AM
8 AM
9 AM
10 AM
11 AM
12 PM
1 PM
2 PM
3 PM
4 PM
5 PM
6 PM
7 PM
8 PM
9 PM

Top 3 Goals I'm Setting for Myself Today:
_____
_____
_____

Words & Affirmations I'm Empowering Myself With Today:
_____
_____
_____

Ways I'm Motivating Myself Today:
_____
_____
_____

Ways I'm Bringing Joy into My Day Today:
_____
_____
_____

My Week in Review

Accomplishments I'm Most Proud of This Week:
_____
_____
_____
_____

Obstacles & Challenges I Triumphed Over This Week:
_____
_____
_____
_____

Ways I Was Kind To Myself & Others This Week:
_____
_____
_____
_____

What I'm Most Grateful For This Week:
_____
_____
_____
_____

Engage Your Goals!

Week #39

"Most of the important things in the world have been accomplished by people who have kept on trying when there seemed to be no help at all."
~ Dale Carnegie

Revelations From The Research:

Van Yperen, Blaga, & Postmes discovered that pursuing education and work-related goals focused on mastery and high performance propels successful performance, whereas setting goals that focus on avoiding failure are associated with negative performance.[39]

3 Ps Weekly Action Agenda

Week of _____
                              Date

Professional:		**Personal:**		**Passions:**	
Actions	Complete By	Actions	Complete By	Actions	Complete By

Longer Term Actions or Projects:

Commitment Calendar

Sunday _____

Date

5 AM	**Top 3 Goals I'm Setting for Myself Today:**
6 AM	_____
7 AM	_____
8 AM	_____
9 AM	**Words & Affirmations I'm Empowering Myself With Today:**
10 AM	_____
11 AM	_____
12 PM	_____
1 PM	**Ways I'm Motivating Myself Today:**
2 PM	_____
3 PM	_____
4 PM	_____
5 PM	**Ways I'm Bringing Joy into My Day Today:**
6 PM	_____
7 PM	_____
8 PM	_____
9 PM	

Monday _____

Date

5 AM	**Top 3 Goals I'm Setting for Myself Today:**
6 AM	_____
7 AM	_____
8 AM	_____
9 AM	**Words & Affirmations I'm Empowering Myself With Today:**
10 AM	_____
11 AM	_____
12 PM	_____
1 PM	**Ways I'm Motivating Myself Today:**
2 PM	_____
3 PM	_____
4 PM	_____
5 PM	**Ways I'm Bringing Joy into My Day Today:**
6 PM	_____
7 PM	_____
8 PM	_____
9 PM	

Tuesday _____
Date

Time	
5 AM	
6 AM	
7 AM	
8 AM	
9 AM	
10 AM	
11 AM	
12 PM	
1 PM	
2 PM	
3 PM	
4 PM	
5 PM	
6 PM	
7 PM	
8 PM	
9 PM	

Top 3 Goals I'm Setting for Myself Today:
_____
_____
_____

Words & Affirmations I'm Empowering Myself With Today:
_____
_____
_____

Ways I'm Motivating Myself Today:
_____
_____
_____

Ways I'm Bringing Joy into My Day Today:
_____
_____
_____

Wednesday _____
Date

Time	
5 AM	
6 AM	
7 AM	
8 AM	
9 AM	
10 AM	
11 AM	
12 PM	
1 PM	
2 PM	
3 PM	
4 PM	
5 PM	
6 PM	
7 PM	
8 PM	
9 PM	

Top 3 Goals I'm Setting for Myself Today:
_____
_____
_____

Words & Affirmations I'm Empowering Myself With Today:
_____
_____
_____

Ways I'm Motivating Myself Today:
_____
_____
_____

Ways I'm Bringing Joy into My Day Today:
_____
_____
_____

Thursday _____
Date

Time	
5 AM	
6 AM	
7 AM	
8 AM	

Top 3 Goals I'm Setting for Myself Today:
_____
_____
_____

9 AM	
10 AM	
11 AM	
12 PM	

Words & Affirmations I'm Empowering Myself With Today:
_____
_____
_____

1 PM	
2 PM	
3 PM	
4 PM	

Ways I'm Motivating Myself Today:
_____
_____
_____

5 PM	
6 PM	
7 PM	
8 PM	
9 PM	

Ways I'm Bringing Joy into My Day Today:
_____
_____
_____

Friday _____
Date

Time	
5 AM	
6 AM	
7 AM	
8 AM	

Top 3 Goals I'm Setting for Myself Today:
_____
_____
_____

9 AM	
10 AM	
11 AM	
12 PM	

Words & Affirmations I'm Empowering Myself With Today:
_____
_____
_____

1 PM	
2 PM	
3 PM	
4 PM	

Ways I'm Motivating Myself Today:
_____
_____
_____

5 PM	
6 PM	
7 PM	
8 PM	
9 PM	

Ways I'm Bringing Joy into My Day Today:
_____
_____
_____

Saturday _____
                              Date

Time	
5 AM	
6 AM	
7 AM	
8 AM	
9 AM	
10 AM	
11 AM	
12 PM	
1 PM	
2 PM	
3 PM	
4 PM	
5 PM	
6 PM	
7 PM	
8 PM	
9 PM	

Top 3 Goals I'm Setting for Myself Today:
_____
_____
_____

Words & Affirmations I'm Empowering Myself With Today:
_____
_____
_____

Ways I'm Motivating Myself Today:
_____
_____
_____

Ways I'm Bringing Joy into My Day Today:
_____
_____
_____

My Week in Review

Accomplishments I'm Most Proud of This Week:
_____
_____
_____

Obstacles & Challenges I Triumphed Over This Week:
_____
_____
_____

Ways I Was Kind To Myself & Others This Week:
_____
_____
_____

What I'm Most Grateful For This Week:
_____
_____
_____

Engage Your Goals!

Week #40

"You measure the size of the accomplishment by the obstacles you had to overcome to reach your goals."
~ Booker T. Washington

Revelations From The Research:

Hafner, Oberst, & Stock led a 4-week goal setting program where participants developed a goal achievement strategy, outlined steps, anticipated obstacles and ways to overcome them, and imagined how to begin working towards goal achievement. They also engaged in daily task planning and prioritizing, assessing time needed for task completion, implementing concrete steps to reach their goal, and devising implementation intentions (in situation A, I will do B to achieve C). They uncovered that goal setting and time management strategies drive goal directed behavior, facilitate improved allocation of time, and reduce procrastination.[40]

3 Ps Weekly Action Agenda

Week of _____
           Date

Professional: **Personal:**   **Passions:**

Actions   Complete By   Actions   Complete By   Actions   Complete By

Longer Term Actions or Projects:

Commitment Calendar

Sunday _____
Date

5 AM
6 AM
7 AM
8 AM
9 AM
10 AM
11 AM
12 PM
1 PM
2 PM
3 PM
4 PM
5 PM
6 PM
7 PM
8 PM
9 PM

Top 3 Goals I'm Setting for Myself Today:
_____
_____
_____

Words & Affirmations I'm Empowering Myself With Today:
_____
_____
_____

Ways I'm Motivating Myself Today:
_____
_____
_____

Ways I'm Bringing Joy into My Day Today:
_____
_____
_____

Monday _____
Date

5 AM
6 AM
7 AM
8 AM
9 AM
10 AM
11 AM
12 PM
1 PM
2 PM
3 PM
4 PM
5 PM
6 PM
7 PM
8 PM
9 PM

Top 3 Goals I'm Setting for Myself Today:
_____
_____
_____

Words & Affirmations I'm Empowering Myself With Today:
_____
_____
_____

Ways I'm Motivating Myself Today:
_____
_____
_____

Ways I'm Bringing Joy into My Day Today:
_____
_____
_____

Tuesday _____
                              Date

Time	
5 AM	
6 AM	
7 AM	
8 AM	
9 AM	
10 AM	
11 AM	
12 PM	
1 PM	
2 PM	
3 PM	
4 PM	
5 PM	
6 PM	
7 PM	
8 PM	
9 PM	

Top 3 Goals I'm Setting for Myself Today:
_____
_____
_____

Words & Affirmations I'm Empowering Myself With Today:
_____
_____
_____

Ways I'm Motivating Myself Today:
_____
_____
_____

Ways I'm Bringing Joy into My Day Today:
_____
_____
_____

Wednesday _____
                                  Date

Time	
5 AM	
6 AM	
7 AM	
8 AM	
9 AM	
10 AM	
11 AM	
12 PM	
1 PM	
2 PM	
3 PM	
4 PM	
5 PM	
6 PM	
7 PM	
8 PM	
9 PM	

Top 3 Goals I'm Setting for Myself Today:
_____
_____
_____

Words & Affirmations I'm Empowering Myself With Today:
_____
_____
_____

Ways I'm Motivating Myself Today:
_____
_____
_____

Ways I'm Bringing Joy into My Day Today:
_____
_____
_____

Thursday _____
Date

Time	
5 AM	
6 AM	
7 AM	
8 AM	
9 AM	
10 AM	
11 AM	
12 PM	
1 PM	
2 PM	
3 PM	
4 PM	
5 PM	
6 PM	
7 PM	
8 PM	
9 PM	

Top 3 Goals I'm Setting for Myself Today:
_____
_____
_____

Words & Affirmations I'm Empowering Myself With Today:
_____
_____

Ways I'm Motivating Myself Today:
_____
_____

Ways I'm Bringing Joy into My Day Today:
_____
_____

Friday _____
Date

Time	
5 AM	
6 AM	
7 AM	
8 AM	
9 AM	
10 AM	
11 AM	
12 PM	
1 PM	
2 PM	
3 PM	
4 PM	
5 PM	
6 PM	
7 PM	
8 PM	
9 PM	

Top 3 Goals I'm Setting for Myself Today:
_____
_____
_____

Words & Affirmations I'm Empowering Myself With Today:
_____
_____

Ways I'm Motivating Myself Today:
_____
_____

Ways I'm Bringing Joy into My Day Today:
_____
_____

Saturday _____
                              Date

Time	
5 AM	
6 AM	
7 AM	
8 AM	
9 AM	
10 AM	
11 AM	
12 PM	
1 PM	
2 PM	
3 PM	
4 PM	
5 PM	
6 PM	
7 PM	
8 PM	
9 PM	

Top 3 Goals I'm Setting for Myself Today:
_____
_____
_____

Words & Affirmations I'm Empowering Myself With Today:
_____
_____
_____

Ways I'm Motivating Myself Today:
_____
_____
_____

Ways I'm Bringing Joy into My Day Today:
_____
_____
_____

My Week in Review

Accomplishments I'm Most Proud of This Week:
_____
_____
_____
_____

Obstacles & Challenges I Triumphed Over This Week:
_____
_____
_____
_____

Ways I Was Kind To Myself & Others This Week:
_____
_____
_____
_____

What I'm Most Grateful For This Week:
_____
_____
_____
_____

Engage Your Goals!

Week #41

"If you don't like something, change it. If you can't change it, change your attitude."
~ Maya Angelou

Revelations From The Research:

Nelis, Thom, Jones, Hindle, & Clare found that setting realistic and achievable lifestyle goals helps older adults alter their lifestyle to allow them to age more successfully and reduce risk factors associated with dementia.[41]

3 Ps Weekly Action Agenda

Week of _____
           Date

Professional:

Actions   Complete By

Personal:

Actions   Complete By

Passions:

Actions   Complete By

Longer Term Actions or Projects:

Commitment Calendar

Sunday _____
                                    Date

Time	
5 AM	
6 AM	
7 AM	
8 AM	
9 AM	
10 AM	
11 AM	
12 PM	
1 PM	
2 PM	
3 PM	
4 PM	
5 PM	
6 PM	
7 PM	
8 PM	
9 PM	

Top 3 Goals I'm Setting for Myself Today:
_____
_____
_____

Words & Affirmations I'm Empowering Myself With Today:
_____
_____
_____

Ways I'm Motivating Myself Today:
_____
_____
_____

Ways I'm Bringing Joy into My Day Today:
_____
_____
_____

Monday _____
                                    Date

Time	
5 AM	
6 AM	
7 AM	
8 AM	
9 AM	
10 AM	
11 AM	
12 PM	
1 PM	
2 PM	
3 PM	
4 PM	
5 PM	
6 PM	
7 PM	
8 PM	
9 PM	

Top 3 Goals I'm Setting for Myself Today:
_____
_____
_____

Words & Affirmations I'm Empowering Myself With Today:
_____
_____
_____

Ways I'm Motivating Myself Today:
_____
_____
_____

Ways I'm Bringing Joy into My Day Today:
_____
_____
_____

Tuesday _____
Date

Time	
5 AM	
6 AM	
7 AM	
8 AM	
9 AM	
10 AM	
11 AM	
12 PM	
1 PM	
2 PM	
3 PM	
4 PM	
5 PM	
6 PM	
7 PM	
8 PM	
9 PM	

Top 3 Goals I'm Setting for Myself Today:
_____
_____
_____

Words & Affirmations I'm Empowering Myself With Today:
_____
_____
_____

Ways I'm Motivating Myself Today:
_____
_____
_____

Ways I'm Bringing Joy into My Day Today:
_____
_____
_____

Wednesday _____
Date

Time	
5 AM	
6 AM	
7 AM	
8 AM	
9 AM	
10 AM	
11 AM	
12 PM	
1 PM	
2 PM	
3 PM	
4 PM	
5 PM	
6 PM	
7 PM	
8 PM	
9 PM	

Top 3 Goals I'm Setting for Myself Today:
_____
_____
_____

Words & Affirmations I'm Empowering Myself With Today:
_____
_____
_____

Ways I'm Motivating Myself Today:
_____
_____
_____

Ways I'm Bringing Joy into My Day Today:
_____
_____
_____

Thursday _____
Date

Time	
5 AM	
6 AM	
7 AM	
8 AM	
9 AM	
10 AM	
11 AM	
12 PM	
1 PM	
2 PM	
3 PM	
4 PM	
5 PM	
6 PM	
7 PM	
8 PM	
9 PM	

Top 3 Goals I'm Setting for Myself Today:
_____
_____
_____

Words & Affirmations I'm Empowering Myself With Today:
_____
_____
_____

Ways I'm Motivating Myself Today:
_____
_____
_____

Ways I'm Bringing Joy into My Day Today:
_____
_____
_____

Friday _____
Date

Time	
5 AM	
6 AM	
7 AM	
8 AM	
9 AM	
10 AM	
11 AM	
12 PM	
1 PM	
2 PM	
3 PM	
4 PM	
5 PM	
6 PM	
7 PM	
8 PM	
9 PM	

Top 3 Goals I'm Setting for Myself Today:
_____
_____
_____

Words & Affirmations I'm Empowering Myself With Today:
_____
_____
_____

Ways I'm Motivating Myself Today:
_____
_____
_____

Ways I'm Bringing Joy into My Day Today:
_____
_____
_____

Saturday _____
Date

Time	
5 AM	
6 AM	
7 AM	
8 AM	
9 AM	
10 AM	
11 AM	
12 PM	
1 PM	
2 PM	
3 PM	
4 PM	
5 PM	
6 PM	
7 PM	
8 PM	
9 PM	

Top 3 Goals I'm Setting for Myself Today:
_____
_____
_____

Words & Affirmations I'm Empowering Myself With Today:
_____
_____

Ways I'm Motivating Myself Today:
_____
_____

Ways I'm Bringing Joy into My Day Today:
_____
_____

My Week in Review

Accomplishments I'm Most Proud of This Week:
_____
_____
_____

Obstacles & Challenges I Triumphed Over This Week:
_____
_____
_____

Ways I Was Kind To Myself & Others This Week:
_____
_____
_____

What I'm Most Grateful For This Week:
_____
_____
_____

Engage Your Goals!

Week #42

"What you're thinking is what you're becoming."
~ Muhammad Ali

Revelations From The Research:

Blankert & Hamstra conducted a study with tennis players and discovered that engaging in goal visualization exercises improved players' game performance.[42]

3 Ps Weekly Action Agenda

Week of _____
Date

Professional:

Actions	Complete By

Personal:

Actions	Complete By

Passions:

Actions	Complete By

Longer Term Actions or Projects:

Commitment Calendar

Sunday _____
Date

Time	
5 AM	
6 AM	
7 AM	
8 AM	
9 AM	
10 AM	
11 AM	
12 PM	
1 PM	
2 PM	
3 PM	
4 PM	
5 PM	
6 PM	
7 PM	
8 PM	
9 PM	

Top 3 Goals I'm Setting for Myself Today:
_____
_____
_____

Words & Affirmations I'm Empowering Myself With Today:
_____
_____
_____

Ways I'm Motivating Myself Today:
_____
_____
_____

Ways I'm Bringing Joy into My Day Today:
_____
_____
_____

Monday _____
Date

Time	
5 AM	
6 AM	
7 AM	
8 AM	
9 AM	
10 AM	
11 AM	
12 PM	
1 PM	
2 PM	
3 PM	
4 PM	
5 PM	
6 PM	
7 PM	
8 PM	
9 PM	

Top 3 Goals I'm Setting for Myself Today:
_____
_____
_____

Words & Affirmations I'm Empowering Myself With Today:
_____
_____
_____

Ways I'm Motivating Myself Today:
_____
_____
_____

Ways I'm Bringing Joy into My Day Today:
_____
_____
_____

Tuesday _____
Date

Time	
5 AM	
6 AM	
7 AM	
8 AM	
9 AM	
10 AM	
11 AM	
12 PM	
1 PM	
2 PM	
3 PM	
4 PM	
5 PM	
6 PM	
7 PM	
8 PM	
9 PM	

Top 3 Goals I'm Setting for Myself Today:
_____
_____
_____

Words & Affirmations I'm Empowering Myself With Today:
_____
_____
_____

Ways I'm Motivating Myself Today:
_____
_____
_____

Ways I'm Bringing Joy into My Day Today:
_____
_____
_____

Wednesday _____
Date

Time	
5 AM	
6 AM	
7 AM	
8 AM	
9 AM	
10 AM	
11 AM	
12 PM	
1 PM	
2 PM	
3 PM	
4 PM	
5 PM	
6 PM	
7 PM	
8 PM	
9 PM	

Top 3 Goals I'm Setting for Myself Today:
_____
_____
_____

Words & Affirmations I'm Empowering Myself With Today:
_____
_____
_____

Ways I'm Motivating Myself Today:
_____
_____
_____

Ways I'm Bringing Joy into My Day Today:
_____
_____
_____

Thursday _____
Date

5 AM	**Top 3 Goals I'm Setting for Myself Today:**
6 AM	_____
7 AM	_____
8 AM	_____
9 AM	**Words & Affirmations I'm Empowering Myself With Today:**
10 AM	_____
11 AM	_____
12 PM	_____
1 PM	**Ways I'm Motivating Myself Today:**
2 PM	_____
3 PM	_____
4 PM	_____
5 PM	**Ways I'm Bringing Joy into My Day Today:**
6 PM	_____
7 PM	_____
8 PM	_____
9 PM	

Friday _____
Date

5 AM	**Top 3 Goals I'm Setting for Myself Today:**
6 AM	_____
7 AM	_____
8 AM	_____
9 AM	**Words & Affirmations I'm Empowering Myself With Today:**
10 AM	_____
11 AM	_____
12 PM	_____
1 PM	**Ways I'm Motivating Myself Today:**
2 PM	_____
3 PM	_____
4 PM	_____
5 PM	**Ways I'm Bringing Joy into My Day Today:**
6 PM	_____
7 PM	_____
8 PM	_____
9 PM	

Saturday _____
Date

5 AM	**Top 3 Goals I'm Setting for Myself Today:**
6 AM	_____
7 AM	_____
8 AM	_____
9 AM	**Words & Affirmations I'm Empowering Myself With Today:**
10 AM	_____
11 AM	_____
12 PM	_____
1 PM	**Ways I'm Motivating Myself Today:**
2 PM	_____
3 PM	_____
4 PM	_____
5 PM	**Ways I'm Bringing Joy into My Day Today:**
6 PM	_____
7 PM	_____
8 PM	_____
9 PM	

My Week in Review

Accomplishments I'm Most Proud of This Week:
_____
_____
_____

Obstacles & Challenges I Triumphed Over This Week:
_____
_____
_____

Ways I Was Kind To Myself & Others This Week:
_____
_____
_____

What I'm Most Grateful For This Week:
_____
_____
_____

Engage Your Goals!

Week #43

"Instead of looking at the past, I put myself ahead twenty years and try to look at what I need to do now in order to get there then."
~ Diana Ross

Revelations From The Research:

Van Eerde conducted a study of employees participating in a workplace time management training program and found that training participants reported a significant decrease in avoidance behavior and worry, as well as an increase in their ability to manage their time and avoid procrastination behaviors.[43]

3 Ps Weekly Action Agenda

Week of _____
                    Date

Professional:

Actions   Complete By

Personal:

Actions   Complete By

Passions:

Actions   Complete By

Longer Term Actions or Projects:

Commitment Calendar

Sunday _____
                                    Date

Time	
5 AM	
6 AM	
7 AM	
8 AM	
9 AM	
10 AM	
11 AM	
12 PM	
1 PM	
2 PM	
3 PM	
4 PM	
5 PM	
6 PM	
7 PM	
8 PM	
9 PM	

Top 3 Goals I'm Setting for Myself Today:
_____
_____
_____

Words & Affirmations I'm Empowering Myself With Today:
_____
_____
_____

Ways I'm Motivating Myself Today:
_____
_____
_____

Ways I'm Bringing Joy into My Day Today:
_____
_____
_____

Monday _____
                                    Date

Time	
5 AM	
6 AM	
7 AM	
8 AM	
9 AM	
10 AM	
11 AM	
12 PM	
1 PM	
2 PM	
3 PM	
4 PM	
5 PM	
6 PM	
7 PM	
8 PM	
9 PM	

Top 3 Goals I'm Setting for Myself Today:
_____
_____
_____

Words & Affirmations I'm Empowering Myself With Today:
_____
_____
_____

Ways I'm Motivating Myself Today:
_____
_____
_____

Ways I'm Bringing Joy into My Day Today:
_____
_____
_____

Tuesday _____
Date

Time	
5 AM	
6 AM	
7 AM	
8 AM	
9 AM	
10 AM	
11 AM	
12 PM	
1 PM	
2 PM	
3 PM	
4 PM	
5 PM	
6 PM	
7 PM	
8 PM	
9 PM	

Top 3 Goals I'm Setting for Myself Today:
_____
_____
_____

Words & Affirmations I'm Empowering Myself With Today:
_____
_____
_____

Ways I'm Motivating Myself Today:
_____
_____
_____

Ways I'm Bringing Joy into My Day Today:
_____
_____
_____

Wednesday _____
Date

Time	
5 AM	
6 AM	
7 AM	
8 AM	
9 AM	
10 AM	
11 AM	
12 PM	
1 PM	
2 PM	
3 PM	
4 PM	
5 PM	
6 PM	
7 PM	
8 PM	
9 PM	

Top 3 Goals I'm Setting for Myself Today:
_____
_____
_____

Words & Affirmations I'm Empowering Myself With Today:
_____
_____
_____

Ways I'm Motivating Myself Today:
_____
_____
_____

Ways I'm Bringing Joy into My Day Today:
_____
_____
_____

Thursday _____
Date

5 AM	
6 AM	
7 AM	
8 AM	
9 AM	
10 AM	
11 AM	
12 PM	
1 PM	
2 PM	
3 PM	
4 PM	
5 PM	
6 PM	
7 PM	
8 PM	
9 PM	

Top 3 Goals I'm Setting for Myself Today:
_____
_____
_____

Words & Affirmations I'm Empowering Myself With Today:
_____
_____
_____

Ways I'm Motivating Myself Today:
_____
_____
_____

Ways I'm Bringing Joy into My Day Today:
_____
_____
_____

Friday _____
Date

5 AM	
6 AM	
7 AM	
8 AM	
9 AM	
10 AM	
11 AM	
12 PM	
1 PM	
2 PM	
3 PM	
4 PM	
5 PM	
6 PM	
7 PM	
8 PM	
9 PM	

Top 3 Goals I'm Setting for Myself Today:
_____
_____
_____

Words & Affirmations I'm Empowering Myself With Today:
_____
_____
_____

Ways I'm Motivating Myself Today:
_____
_____
_____

Ways I'm Bringing Joy into My Day Today:
_____
_____
_____

Saturday _____
Date

5 AM
6 AM
7 AM
8 AM
9 AM
10 AM
11 AM
12 PM
1 PM
2 PM
3 PM
4 PM
5 PM
6 PM
7 PM
8 PM
9 PM

Top 3 Goals I'm Setting for Myself Today:
_____
_____
_____

Words & Affirmations I'm Empowering Myself With Today:
_____
_____
_____

Ways I'm Motivating Myself Today:
_____
_____
_____

Ways I'm Bringing Joy into My Day Today:
_____
_____
_____

My Week in Review

Accomplishments I'm Most Proud of This Week:
_____
_____
_____

Obstacles & Challenges I Triumphed Over This Week:
_____
_____
_____

Ways I Was Kind To Myself & Others This Week:
_____
_____
_____

What I'm Most Grateful For This Week:
_____
_____
_____

Engage Your Goals!

Week #44

"What would you do if you weren't afraid."
~ Spencer Johnson

Revelations From The Research:

Dominick & Cole discovered that people who think of their personal goals as identities are more likely to engage in goal-consistent behavior. Specifically, they found that individuals with stronger healthy-eater identities made healthier food choices, felt their goals were easier to pursue, and experienced greater success in managing their goals.[44]

3 Ps Weekly Action Agenda

Week of _____
Date

Professional:

Actions	Complete By

Personal:

Actions	Complete By

Passions:

Actions	Complete By

Longer Term Actions or Projects:

Commitment Calendar

Sunday _____
                                            Date

Top 3 Goals I'm Setting for Myself Today:
_____
_____
_____

Words & Affirmations I'm Empowering Myself With Today:
_____
_____
_____

Ways I'm Motivating Myself Today:
_____
_____
_____

Ways I'm Bringing Joy into My Day Today:
_____
_____
_____
_____

- 5 AM
- 6 AM
- 7 AM
- 8 AM
- 9 AM
- 10 AM
- 11 AM
- 12 PM
- 1 PM
- 2 PM
- 3 PM
- 4 PM
- 5 PM
- 6 PM
- 7 PM
- 8 PM
- 9 PM

Monday _____
                                            Date

Top 3 Goals I'm Setting for Myself Today:
_____
_____
_____

Words & Affirmations I'm Empowering Myself With Today:
_____
_____
_____

Ways I'm Motivating Myself Today:
_____
_____
_____

Ways I'm Bringing Joy into My Day Today:
_____
_____
_____
_____

- 5 AM
- 6 AM
- 7 AM
- 8 AM
- 9 AM
- 10 AM
- 11 AM
- 12 PM
- 1 PM
- 2 PM
- 3 PM
- 4 PM
- 5 PM
- 6 PM
- 7 PM
- 8 PM
- 9 PM

Tuesday _____
Date

5 AM	
6 AM	
7 AM	
8 AM	
9 AM	
10 AM	
11 AM	
12 PM	
1 PM	
2 PM	
3 PM	
4 PM	
5 PM	
6 PM	
7 PM	
8 PM	
9 PM	

Top 3 Goals I'm Setting for Myself Today:
_____
_____
_____

Words & Affirmations I'm Empowering Myself With Today:
_____
_____
_____

Ways I'm Motivating Myself Today:
_____
_____
_____

Ways I'm Bringing Joy into My Day Today:
_____
_____
_____

Wednesday _____
Date

5 AM	
6 AM	
7 AM	
8 AM	
9 AM	
10 AM	
11 AM	
12 PM	
1 PM	
2 PM	
3 PM	
4 PM	
5 PM	
6 PM	
7 PM	
8 PM	
9 PM	

Top 3 Goals I'm Setting for Myself Today:
_____
_____
_____

Words & Affirmations I'm Empowering Myself With Today:
_____
_____
_____

Ways I'm Motivating Myself Today:
_____
_____
_____

Ways I'm Bringing Joy into My Day Today:
_____
_____
_____

Thursday _____
Date

Time	
5 AM	
6 AM	
7 AM	
8 AM	
9 AM	
10 AM	
11 AM	
12 PM	
1 PM	
2 PM	
3 PM	
4 PM	
5 PM	
6 PM	
7 PM	
8 PM	
9 PM	

Top 3 Goals I'm Setting for Myself Today:
_____
_____
_____

Words & Affirmations I'm Empowering Myself With Today:
_____
_____
_____

Ways I'm Motivating Myself Today:
_____
_____
_____

Ways I'm Bringing Joy into My Day Today:
_____
_____
_____

Friday _____
Date

Time	
5 AM	
6 AM	
7 AM	
8 AM	
9 AM	
10 AM	
11 AM	
12 PM	
1 PM	
2 PM	
3 PM	
4 PM	
5 PM	
6 PM	
7 PM	
8 PM	
9 PM	

Top 3 Goals I'm Setting for Myself Today:
_____
_____
_____

Words & Affirmations I'm Empowering Myself With Today:
_____
_____
_____

Ways I'm Motivating Myself Today:
_____
_____
_____

Ways I'm Bringing Joy into My Day Today:
_____
_____
_____

Saturday _____
Date

5 AM
6 AM
7 AM
8 AM
9 AM
10 AM
11 AM
12 PM
1 PM
2 PM
3 PM
4 PM
5 PM
6 PM
7 PM
8 PM
9 PM

Top 3 Goals I'm Setting for Myself Today:
_____
_____
_____

Words & Affirmations I'm Empowering Myself With Today:
_____
_____
_____

Ways I'm Motivating Myself Today:
_____
_____
_____

Ways I'm Bringing Joy into My Day Today:
_____
_____
_____

My Week in Review

Accomplishments I'm Most Proud of This Week:
_____
_____
_____

Obstacles & Challenges I Triumphed Over This Week:
_____
_____
_____

Ways I Was Kind To Myself & Others This Week:
_____
_____
_____

What I'm Most Grateful For This Week:
_____
_____
_____

Engage Your Goals!

Week #45

"I have discovered in life that there are ways of getting almost anywhere you want to go, if you really want to go."
~ Langston Hughes

Revelations From The Research:

Ogawa, Omon, Yuda, Ishigaki, Imai, Ohmatsu, & Morioka conducted a 4-week goal setting program with patients in a subacute rehabilitation ward, having them set specific goals related to residential and domestic arrangements, personal care, leisure, work, relationships, life philosophy, and finances. Patients then selected their top three priority goals. The study revealed that patients who set life goals were more actively engaged in their rehabilitation treatment program and experienced less anxiety and greater emotional wellbeing.[45]

3 Ps Weekly Action Agenda

Week of _____
                        Date

Professional:

Actions	Complete By

Personal:

Actions	Complete By

Passions:

Actions	Complete By

Longer Term Actions or Projects:

Commitment Calendar

Sunday _____

Date _____

5 AM
6 AM
7 AM
8 AM
9 AM
10 AM
11 AM
12 PM
1 PM
2 PM
3 PM
4 PM
5 PM
6 PM
7 PM
8 PM
9 PM

Top 3 Goals I'm Setting for Myself Today:
_____
_____
_____

Words & Affirmations I'm Empowering Myself With Today:
_____
_____
_____

Ways I'm Motivating Myself Today:
_____
_____
_____

Ways I'm Bringing Joy into My Day Today:
_____
_____
_____

Monday _____

Date _____

5 AM
6 AM
7 AM
8 AM
9 AM
10 AM
11 AM
12 PM
1 PM
2 PM
3 PM
4 PM
5 PM
6 PM
7 PM
8 PM
9 PM

Top 3 Goals I'm Setting for Myself Today:
_____
_____
_____

Words & Affirmations I'm Empowering Myself With Today:
_____
_____
_____

Ways I'm Motivating Myself Today:
_____
_____
_____

Ways I'm Bringing Joy into My Day Today:
_____
_____
_____

Tuesday _____
Date

Time	
5 AM	
6 AM	
7 AM	
8 AM	
9 AM	
10 AM	
11 AM	
12 PM	
1 PM	
2 PM	
3 PM	
4 PM	
5 PM	
6 PM	
7 PM	
8 PM	
9 PM	

Top 3 Goals I'm Setting for Myself Today:
_____
_____
_____

Words & Affirmations I'm Empowering Myself With Today:
_____
_____
_____

Ways I'm Motivating Myself Today:
_____
_____
_____

Ways I'm Bringing Joy into My Day Today:
_____
_____
_____
_____

Wednesday _____
Date

Time	
5 AM	
6 AM	
7 AM	
8 AM	
9 AM	
10 AM	
11 AM	
12 PM	
1 PM	
2 PM	
3 PM	
4 PM	
5 PM	
6 PM	
7 PM	
8 PM	
9 PM	

Top 3 Goals I'm Setting for Myself Today:
_____
_____
_____

Words & Affirmations I'm Empowering Myself With Today:
_____
_____
_____

Ways I'm Motivating Myself Today:
_____
_____
_____

Ways I'm Bringing Joy into My Day Today:
_____
_____
_____
_____

Thursday _____
Date

Time	
5 AM	
6 AM	
7 AM	
8 AM	
9 AM	
10 AM	
11 AM	
12 PM	
1 PM	
2 PM	
3 PM	
4 PM	
5 PM	
6 PM	
7 PM	
8 PM	
9 PM	

Top 3 Goals I'm Setting for Myself Today:
_____
_____
_____

Words & Affirmations I'm Empowering Myself With Today:
_____
_____
_____

Ways I'm Motivating Myself Today:
_____
_____
_____

Ways I'm Bringing Joy into My Day Today:
_____
_____
_____

Friday _____
Date

Time	
5 AM	
6 AM	
7 AM	
8 AM	
9 AM	
10 AM	
11 AM	
12 PM	
1 PM	
2 PM	
3 PM	
4 PM	
5 PM	
6 PM	
7 PM	
8 PM	
9 PM	

Top 3 Goals I'm Setting for Myself Today:
_____
_____
_____

Words & Affirmations I'm Empowering Myself With Today:
_____
_____
_____

Ways I'm Motivating Myself Today:
_____
_____
_____

Ways I'm Bringing Joy into My Day Today:
_____
_____
_____

Saturday _____
                           Date

5 AM	**Top 3 Goals I'm Setting for Myself Today:**
6 AM	
7 AM	
8 AM	
9 AM	**Words & Affirmations I'm Empowering Myself With Today:**
10 AM	
11 AM	
12 PM	
1 PM	**Ways I'm Motivating Myself Today:**
2 PM	
3 PM	
4 PM	
5 PM	**Ways I'm Bringing Joy into My Day Today:**
6 PM	
7 PM	
8 PM	
9 PM	

My Week in Review

Accomplishments I'm Most Proud of This Week:
_____
_____
_____

Obstacles & Challenges I Triumphed Over This Week:
_____
_____
_____

Ways I Was Kind To Myself & Others This Week:
_____
_____
_____

What I'm Most Grateful For This Week:
_____
_____
_____

Engage Your Goals!

Week #46

"I am lucky that whatever fear I have inside me, my desire to win is always stronger."
~ Serena Williams

Revelations From The Research:

Oliver & MacLeod conducted an online self-help goal-setting and planning intervention with working adults and found that goal setting and planning facilitates positive emotions, flourishing, and life satisfaction.[46]

3 Ps Weekly Action Agenda

Week of _____
            Date

Professional:

Actions   Complete By

Personal:

Actions   Complete By

Passions:

Actions   Complete By

Longer Term Actions or Projects:

Commitment Calendar

Sunday _____
Date

5 AM
6 AM
7 AM
8 AM
9 AM
10 AM
11 AM
12 PM
1 PM
2 PM
3 PM
4 PM
5 PM
6 PM
7 PM
8 PM
9 PM

Top 3 Goals I'm Setting for Myself Today:
_____
_____
_____

Words & Affirmations I'm Empowering Myself With Today:
_____
_____
_____

Ways I'm Motivating Myself Today:
_____
_____
_____

Ways I'm Bringing Joy into My Day Today:
_____
_____
_____

Monday _____
Date

5 AM
6 AM
7 AM
8 AM
9 AM
10 AM
11 AM
12 PM
1 PM
2 PM
3 PM
4 PM
5 PM
6 PM
7 PM
8 PM
9 PM

Top 3 Goals I'm Setting for Myself Today:
_____
_____
_____

Words & Affirmations I'm Empowering Myself With Today:
_____
_____
_____

Ways I'm Motivating Myself Today:
_____
_____
_____

Ways I'm Bringing Joy into My Day Today:
_____
_____
_____

Tuesday _____
Date

5 AM	
6 AM	
7 AM	
8 AM	
9 AM	
10 AM	
11 AM	
12 PM	
1 PM	
2 PM	
3 PM	
4 PM	
5 PM	
6 PM	
7 PM	
8 PM	
9 PM	

Top 3 Goals I'm Setting for Myself Today:
_____
_____
_____

Words & Affirmations I'm Empowering Myself With Today:
_____
_____
_____

Ways I'm Motivating Myself Today:
_____
_____
_____

Ways I'm Bringing Joy into My Day Today:
_____
_____
_____

Wednesday _____
Date

5 AM	
6 AM	
7 AM	
8 AM	
9 AM	
10 AM	
11 AM	
12 PM	
1 PM	
2 PM	
3 PM	
4 PM	
5 PM	
6 PM	
7 PM	
8 PM	
9 PM	

Top 3 Goals I'm Setting for Myself Today:
_____
_____
_____

Words & Affirmations I'm Empowering Myself With Today:
_____
_____
_____

Ways I'm Motivating Myself Today:
_____
_____
_____

Ways I'm Bringing Joy into My Day Today:
_____
_____
_____

Thursday _____
_____ Date

5 AM	
6 AM	
7 AM	
8 AM	
9 AM	
10 AM	
11 AM	
12 PM	
1 PM	
2 PM	
3 PM	
4 PM	
5 PM	
6 PM	
7 PM	
8 PM	
9 PM	

Top 3 Goals I'm Setting for Myself Today:
_____
_____
_____

Words & Affirmations I'm Empowering Myself With Today:
_____
_____
_____

Ways I'm Motivating Myself Today:
_____
_____
_____

Ways I'm Bringing Joy into My Day Today:
_____
_____
_____

Friday _____
_____ Date

5 AM	
6 AM	
7 AM	
8 AM	
9 AM	
10 AM	
11 AM	
12 PM	
1 PM	
2 PM	
3 PM	
4 PM	
5 PM	
6 PM	
7 PM	
8 PM	
9 PM	

Top 3 Goals I'm Setting for Myself Today:
_____
_____
_____

Words & Affirmations I'm Empowering Myself With Today:
_____
_____
_____

Ways I'm Motivating Myself Today:
_____
_____
_____

Ways I'm Bringing Joy into My Day Today:
_____
_____
_____

Saturday _____

Date

5 AM	
6 AM	**Top 3 Goals I'm Setting for Myself Today:**
7 AM	_____
8 AM	_____
9 AM	_____
10 AM	**Words & Affirmations I'm Empowering Myself With Today:**
11 AM	_____
12 PM	_____
1 PM	**Ways I'm Motivating Myself Today:**
2 PM	_____
3 PM	_____
4 PM	_____
5 PM	**Ways I'm Bringing Joy into My Day Today:**
6 PM	_____
7 PM	_____
8 PM	_____
9 PM	

My Week in Review

Accomplishments I'm Most Proud of This Week:
_____
_____
_____

Obstacles & Challenges I Triumphed Over This Week:
_____
_____
_____

Ways I Was Kind To Myself & Others This Week:
_____
_____
_____

What I'm Most Grateful For This Week:
_____
_____
_____

Engage Your Goals!

Week #47

"Failure is the condiment that gives success its flavor."
~ Truman Capote

Revelations From The Research:

Zampetakis, Bouranta, & Moustakis found that creativity (devising innovative ideas and solutions) is facilitated by daily planning and time management behaviors, confidence in long-range planning, perceived control of time, and tenacity.[47]

3 Ps Weekly Action Agenda

Week of _____
Date

Professional:

Actions   Complete By

Personal:

Actions   Complete By

Passions:

Actions   Complete By

Longer Term Actions or Projects:

Commitment Calendar

Sunday _____
Date

5 AM
6 AM
7 AM
8 AM
9 AM
10 AM
11 AM
12 PM
1 PM
2 PM
3 PM
4 PM
5 PM
6 PM
7 PM
8 PM
9 PM

Top 3 Goals I'm Setting for Myself Today:
_____
_____
_____

Words & Affirmations I'm Empowering Myself With Today:
_____
_____
_____

Ways I'm Motivating Myself Today:
_____
_____
_____

Ways I'm Bringing Joy into My Day Today:
_____
_____
_____

Monday _____
Date

5 AM
6 AM
7 AM
8 AM
9 AM
10 AM
11 AM
12 PM
1 PM
2 PM
3 PM
4 PM
5 PM
6 PM
7 PM
8 PM
9 PM

Top 3 Goals I'm Setting for Myself Today:
_____
_____
_____

Words & Affirmations I'm Empowering Myself With Today:
_____
_____
_____

Ways I'm Motivating Myself Today:
_____
_____
_____

Ways I'm Bringing Joy into My Day Today:
_____
_____
_____

Tuesday _____
                              Date

5 AM
6 AM
7 AM
8 AM
9 AM
10 AM
11 AM
12 PM
1 PM
2 PM
3 PM
4 PM
5 PM
6 PM
7 PM
8 PM
9 PM

Top 3 Goals I'm Setting for Myself Today:
_____
_____
_____

Words & Affirmations I'm Empowering Myself With Today:
_____
_____
_____

Ways I'm Motivating Myself Today:
_____
_____
_____

Ways I'm Bringing Joy into My Day Today:
_____
_____
_____

Wednesday _____
                              Date

5 AM
6 AM
7 AM
8 AM
9 AM
10 AM
11 AM
12 PM
1 PM
2 PM
3 PM
4 PM
5 PM
6 PM
7 PM
8 PM
9 PM

Top 3 Goals I'm Setting for Myself Today:
_____
_____
_____

Words & Affirmations I'm Empowering Myself With Today:
_____
_____
_____

Ways I'm Motivating Myself Today:
_____
_____
_____

Ways I'm Bringing Joy into My Day Today:
_____
_____
_____

Thursday _____
Date

5 AM	
6 AM	
7 AM	
8 AM	
9 AM	
10 AM	
11 AM	
12 PM	
1 PM	
2 PM	
3 PM	
4 PM	
5 PM	
6 PM	
7 PM	
8 PM	
9 PM	

Top 3 Goals I'm Setting for Myself Today:
_____
_____
_____

Words & Affirmations I'm Empowering Myself With Today:
_____
_____
_____

Ways I'm Motivating Myself Today:
_____
_____
_____

Ways I'm Bringing Joy into My Day Today:
_____
_____
_____

Friday _____
Date

5 AM	
6 AM	
7 AM	
8 AM	
9 AM	
10 AM	
11 AM	
12 PM	
1 PM	
2 PM	
3 PM	
4 PM	
5 PM	
6 PM	
7 PM	
8 PM	
9 PM	

Top 3 Goals I'm Setting for Myself Today:
_____
_____
_____

Words & Affirmations I'm Empowering Myself With Today:
_____
_____
_____

Ways I'm Motivating Myself Today:
_____
_____
_____

Ways I'm Bringing Joy into My Day Today:
_____
_____
_____

Saturday _____
Date

5 AM	
6 AM	
7 AM	
8 AM	
9 AM	
10 AM	
11 AM	
12 PM	
1 PM	
2 PM	
3 PM	
4 PM	
5 PM	
6 PM	
7 PM	
8 PM	
9 PM	

Top 3 Goals I'm Setting for Myself Today:
_____
_____
_____

Words & Affirmations I'm Empowering Myself With Today:
_____
_____
_____

Ways I'm Motivating Myself Today:
_____
_____
_____

Ways I'm Bringing Joy into My Day Today:
_____
_____
_____

My Week in Review

Accomplishments I'm Most Proud of This Week:
_____
_____
_____

Obstacles & Challenges I Triumphed Over This Week:
_____
_____
_____

Ways I Was Kind To Myself & Others This Week:
_____
_____
_____

What I'm Most Grateful For This Week:
_____
_____
_____

Engage Your Goals!

Week #48

"Dreams do not come true just because you dream them. It's hard work that makes things happen. It's hard work that creates change."
~ Shonda Rhimes

Revelations From The Research:

Koole, Smeets, van Knippenberg, & Dijksterhuis found that after failing to complete a goal, participants who were given time to engage in self-affirmation experienced significantly reduced negative rumination, as well as increased positive emotions.[48]

3 Ps Weekly Action Agenda

Week of _____
Date

Professional:

Actions   Complete By

Personal:

Actions   Complete By

Passions:

Actions   Complete By

Longer Term Actions or Projects:

Commitment Calendar

Sunday _____

Date

Time	
5 AM	
6 AM	
7 AM	
8 AM	
9 AM	
10 AM	
11 AM	
12 PM	
1 PM	
2 PM	
3 PM	
4 PM	
5 PM	
6 PM	
7 PM	
8 PM	
9 PM	

Top 3 Goals I'm Setting for Myself Today:
_____
_____
_____

Words & Affirmations I'm Empowering Myself With Today:
_____
_____
_____

Ways I'm Motivating Myself Today:
_____
_____
_____

Ways I'm Bringing Joy into My Day Today:
_____
_____
_____

Monday _____

Date

Time	
5 AM	
6 AM	
7 AM	
8 AM	
9 AM	
10 AM	
11 AM	
12 PM	
1 PM	
2 PM	
3 PM	
4 PM	
5 PM	
6 PM	
7 PM	
8 PM	
9 PM	

Top 3 Goals I'm Setting for Myself Today:
_____
_____
_____

Words & Affirmations I'm Empowering Myself With Today:
_____
_____
_____

Ways I'm Motivating Myself Today:
_____
_____
_____

Ways I'm Bringing Joy into My Day Today:
_____
_____
_____

Tuesday _____
Date

Time	
5 AM	
6 AM	
7 AM	
8 AM	
9 AM	
10 AM	
11 AM	
12 PM	
1 PM	
2 PM	
3 PM	
4 PM	
5 PM	
6 PM	
7 PM	
8 PM	
9 PM	

Top 3 Goals I'm Setting for Myself Today:
_____
_____
_____

Words & Affirmations I'm Empowering Myself With Today:
_____
_____
_____

Ways I'm Motivating Myself Today:
_____
_____
_____

Ways I'm Bringing Joy into My Day Today:
_____
_____
_____

Wednesday _____
Date

Time	
5 AM	
6 AM	
7 AM	
8 AM	
9 AM	
10 AM	
11 AM	
12 PM	
1 PM	
2 PM	
3 PM	
4 PM	
5 PM	
6 PM	
7 PM	
8 PM	
9 PM	

Top 3 Goals I'm Setting for Myself Today:
_____
_____
_____

Words & Affirmations I'm Empowering Myself With Today:
_____
_____
_____

Ways I'm Motivating Myself Today:
_____
_____
_____

Ways I'm Bringing Joy into My Day Today:
_____
_____
_____

Thursday _____
                                    Date

Time	
5 AM	
6 AM	
7 AM	
8 AM	
9 AM	
10 AM	
11 AM	
12 PM	
1 PM	
2 PM	
3 PM	
4 PM	
5 PM	
6 PM	
7 PM	
8 PM	
9 PM	

Top 3 Goals I'm Setting for Myself Today:
_____
_____
_____

Words & Affirmations I'm Empowering Myself With Today:
_____
_____
_____

Ways I'm Motivating Myself Today:
_____
_____
_____

Ways I'm Bringing Joy into My Day Today:
_____
_____
_____

Friday _____
                                    Date

Time	
5 AM	
6 AM	
7 AM	
8 AM	
9 AM	
10 AM	
11 AM	
12 PM	
1 PM	
2 PM	
3 PM	
4 PM	
5 PM	
6 PM	
7 PM	
8 PM	
9 PM	

Top 3 Goals I'm Setting for Myself Today:
_____
_____
_____

Words & Affirmations I'm Empowering Myself With Today:
_____
_____
_____

Ways I'm Motivating Myself Today:
_____
_____
_____

Ways I'm Bringing Joy into My Day Today:
_____
_____
_____

Saturday _____
Date

Time	
5 AM	
6 AM	
7 AM	
8 AM	
9 AM	
10 AM	
11 AM	
12 PM	
1 PM	
2 PM	
3 PM	
4 PM	
5 PM	
6 PM	
7 PM	
8 PM	
9 PM	

Top 3 Goals I'm Setting for Myself Today:
_____
_____
_____

Words & Affirmations I'm Empowering Myself With Today:
_____
_____

Ways I'm Motivating Myself Today:
_____
_____

Ways I'm Bringing Joy into My Day Today:
_____
_____

My Week in Review

Accomplishments I'm Most Proud of This Week:
_____
_____
_____

Obstacles & Challenges I Triumphed Over This Week:
_____
_____
_____

Ways I Was Kind To Myself & Others This Week:
_____
_____
_____

What I'm Most Grateful For This Week:
_____
_____
_____

Engage Your Goals!

Week #49

"You don't make progress by standing on the sidelines, whimpering and complaining. You make progress by implementing ideas."
~ Shirley Chisholm

Revelations From The Research:

Masicampo & Baumeister found that those who devise a specific plan to work toward completing an unfinished goal were able to eliminate intrusive thoughts about the unfinished goal and improve performance on both goal-related and unrelated tasks.[49]

3 Ps Weekly Action Agenda

Week of _____
         Date

Professional:

Actions   Complete By

Personal:

Actions   Complete By

Passions:

Actions   Complete By

Longer Term Actions or Projects:

Commitment Calendar

Sunday _____
Date

5 AM	**Top 3 Goals I'm Setting for Myself Today:**
6 AM	_____
7 AM	_____
8 AM	_____
9 AM	**Words & Affirmations I'm Empowering Myself With Today:**
10 AM	_____
11 AM	_____
12 PM	_____
1 PM	**Ways I'm Motivating Myself Today:**
2 PM	_____
3 PM	_____
4 PM	_____
5 PM	**Ways I'm Bringing Joy into My Day Today:**
6 PM	_____
7 PM	_____
8 PM	_____
9 PM	

Monday _____
Date

5 AM	**Top 3 Goals I'm Setting for Myself Today:**
6 AM	_____
7 AM	_____
8 AM	_____
9 AM	**Words & Affirmations I'm Empowering Myself With Today:**
10 AM	_____
11 AM	_____
12 PM	_____
1 PM	**Ways I'm Motivating Myself Today:**
2 PM	_____
3 PM	_____
4 PM	_____
5 PM	**Ways I'm Bringing Joy into My Day Today:**
6 PM	_____
7 PM	_____
8 PM	_____
9 PM	

Tuesday _____
Date

Time	
5 AM	
6 AM	
7 AM	
8 AM	
9 AM	
10 AM	
11 AM	
12 PM	
1 PM	
2 PM	
3 PM	
4 PM	
5 PM	
6 PM	
7 PM	
8 PM	
9 PM	

Top 3 Goals I'm Setting for Myself Today:
_____
_____
_____

Words & Affirmations I'm Empowering Myself With Today:
_____
_____
_____

Ways I'm Motivating Myself Today:
_____
_____
_____

Ways I'm Bringing Joy into My Day Today:
_____
_____
_____

Wednesday _____
Date

Time	
5 AM	
6 AM	
7 AM	
8 AM	
9 AM	
10 AM	
11 AM	
12 PM	
1 PM	
2 PM	
3 PM	
4 PM	
5 PM	
6 PM	
7 PM	
8 PM	
9 PM	

Top 3 Goals I'm Setting for Myself Today:
_____
_____
_____

Words & Affirmations I'm Empowering Myself With Today:
_____
_____
_____

Ways I'm Motivating Myself Today:
_____
_____
_____

Ways I'm Bringing Joy into My Day Today:
_____
_____
_____

Thursday _____
Date

Time	
5 AM	
6 AM	
7 AM	
8 AM	
9 AM	
10 AM	
11 AM	
12 PM	
1 PM	
2 PM	
3 PM	
4 PM	
5 PM	
6 PM	
7 PM	
8 PM	
9 PM	

Top 3 Goals I'm Setting for Myself Today:
_____
_____
_____

Words & Affirmations I'm Empowering Myself With Today:
_____
_____
_____

Ways I'm Motivating Myself Today:
_____
_____
_____

Ways I'm Bringing Joy into My Day Today:
_____
_____
_____

Friday _____
Date

Time	
5 AM	
6 AM	
7 AM	
8 AM	
9 AM	
10 AM	
11 AM	
12 PM	
1 PM	
2 PM	
3 PM	
4 PM	
5 PM	
6 PM	
7 PM	
8 PM	
9 PM	

Top 3 Goals I'm Setting for Myself Today:
_____
_____
_____

Words & Affirmations I'm Empowering Myself With Today:
_____
_____
_____

Ways I'm Motivating Myself Today:
_____
_____
_____

Ways I'm Bringing Joy into My Day Today:
_____
_____
_____

Saturday _____
Date

Time	
5 AM	
6 AM	
7 AM	
8 AM	
9 AM	
10 AM	
11 AM	
12 PM	
1 PM	
2 PM	
3 PM	
4 PM	
5 PM	
6 PM	
7 PM	
8 PM	
9 PM	

Top 3 Goals I'm Setting for Myself Today:
_____
_____
_____

Words & Affirmations I'm Empowering Myself With Today:
_____
_____

Ways I'm Motivating Myself Today:
_____
_____

Ways I'm Bringing Joy into My Day Today:
_____
_____

My Week in Review

Accomplishments I'm Most Proud of This Week:
_____
_____
_____

Obstacles & Challenges I Triumphed Over This Week:
_____
_____
_____

Ways I Was Kind To Myself & Others This Week:
_____
_____
_____

What I'm Most Grateful For This Week:
_____
_____
_____

Engage Your Goals!

Week #50

*"Change will not come if we wait for some other person or some other time.
We are the ones we've been waiting for.
We are the change that we seek."
~ Barack Obama*

Revelations From The Research:

Kannangara, Allen, Waugh, Nahar, Khan, Rogerson, & Carson discovered that success is associated with passion and perseverance (including having short and long terms goals, resilience, dedication, and endurance), self-control (including time management, self-awareness, prioritizing tasks, and knowing strengths and weaknesses), and positive mindset (including having a positive attitude toward learning and constructive feedback, as well as believing that success is not materialistic).[50]

3 Ps Weekly Action Agenda

Week of _____
               Date

Professional:

Actions   Complete By

Personal:

Actions   Complete By

Passions:

Actions   Complete By

Longer Term Actions or Projects:

Commitment Calendar

Sunday _____
                                    Date

5 AM	Top 3 Goals I'm Setting for Myself Today:
6 AM	_____
7 AM	_____
8 AM	_____
9 AM	Words & Affirmations I'm Empowering Myself With Today:
10 AM	_____
11 AM	_____
12 PM	_____
1 PM	Ways I'm Motivating Myself Today:
2 PM	_____
3 PM	_____
4 PM	_____
5 PM	Ways I'm Bringing Joy into My Day Today:
6 PM	_____
7 PM	_____
8 PM	_____
9 PM	

Monday _____
                                    Date

5 AM	Top 3 Goals I'm Setting for Myself Today:
6 AM	_____
7 AM	_____
8 AM	_____
9 AM	Words & Affirmations I'm Empowering Myself With Today:
10 AM	_____
11 AM	_____
12 PM	_____
1 PM	Ways I'm Motivating Myself Today:
2 PM	_____
3 PM	_____
4 PM	_____
5 PM	Ways I'm Bringing Joy into My Day Today:
6 PM	_____
7 PM	_____
8 PM	_____
9 PM	

Tuesday _____
Date

5 AM
6 AM
7 AM
8 AM
9 AM
10 AM
11 AM
12 PM
1 PM
2 PM
3 PM
4 PM
5 PM
6 PM
7 PM
8 PM
9 PM

Top 3 Goals I'm Setting for Myself Today:
_____
_____
_____

Words & Affirmations I'm Empowering Myself With Today:
_____
_____
_____

Ways I'm Motivating Myself Today:
_____
_____
_____

Ways I'm Bringing Joy into My Day Today:
_____
_____
_____

Wednesday _____
Date

5 AM
6 AM
7 AM
8 AM
9 AM
10 AM
11 AM
12 PM
1 PM
2 PM
3 PM
4 PM
5 PM
6 PM
7 PM
8 PM
9 PM

Top 3 Goals I'm Setting for Myself Today:
_____
_____
_____

Words & Affirmations I'm Empowering Myself With Today:
_____
_____
_____

Ways I'm Motivating Myself Today:
_____
_____
_____

Ways I'm Bringing Joy into My Day Today:
_____
_____
_____

Thursday _____
Date

Time	
5 AM	
6 AM	
7 AM	
8 AM	
9 AM	
10 AM	
11 AM	
12 PM	
1 PM	
2 PM	
3 PM	
4 PM	
5 PM	
6 PM	
7 PM	
8 PM	
9 PM	

Top 3 Goals I'm Setting for Myself Today:
_____
_____
_____

Words & Affirmations I'm Empowering Myself With Today:
_____
_____
_____

Ways I'm Motivating Myself Today:
_____
_____
_____

Ways I'm Bringing Joy into My Day Today:
_____
_____
_____

Friday _____
Date

Time	
5 AM	
6 AM	
7 AM	
8 AM	
9 AM	
10 AM	
11 AM	
12 PM	
1 PM	
2 PM	
3 PM	
4 PM	
5 PM	
6 PM	
7 PM	
8 PM	
9 PM	

Top 3 Goals I'm Setting for Myself Today:
_____
_____
_____

Words & Affirmations I'm Empowering Myself With Today:
_____
_____
_____

Ways I'm Motivating Myself Today:
_____
_____
_____

Ways I'm Bringing Joy into My Day Today:
_____
_____
_____

Saturday _____
                                        Date

Time	
5 AM	
6 AM	
7 AM	
8 AM	
9 AM	
10 AM	
11 AM	
12 PM	
1 PM	
2 PM	
3 PM	
4 PM	
5 PM	
6 PM	
7 PM	
8 PM	
9 PM	

Top 3 Goals I'm Setting for Myself Today:
_____
_____
_____

Words & Affirmations I'm Empowering Myself With Today:
_____
_____
_____

Ways I'm Motivating Myself Today:
_____
_____
_____

Ways I'm Bringing Joy into My Day Today:
_____
_____
_____

My Week in Review

Accomplishments I'm Most Proud of This Week:
_____
_____
_____
_____

Obstacles & Challenges I Triumphed Over This Week:
_____
_____
_____
_____

Ways I Was Kind To Myself & Others This Week:
_____
_____
_____
_____

What I'm Most Grateful For This Week:
_____
_____
_____
_____

Engage Your Goals!

Week #51

"I am deliberate and afraid of nothing."
~ Audre Lorde

Revelations From The Research:

Adhikari & Gollub led a community-based nutrition education program for adults that focused on developing small goal setting and habit formation techniques. They found that goal setting led participants to significantly increase daily physical activity, label reading, healthy food preparation confidence, consumption of vegetables, fruits, and whole grains, as well as decrease soda intake.[51]

3 Ps Weekly Action Agenda

Week of _____
                        Date

Professional:

Actions	Complete By

Personal:

Actions	Complete By

Passions:

Actions	Complete By

Longer Term Actions or Projects:

Commitment Calendar

Sunday _____

Date _____

Time	
5 AM	
6 AM	
7 AM	
8 AM	
9 AM	
10 AM	
11 AM	
12 PM	
1 PM	
2 PM	
3 PM	
4 PM	
5 PM	
6 PM	
7 PM	
8 PM	
9 PM	

Top 3 Goals I'm Setting for Myself Today:
_____
_____
_____

Words & Affirmations I'm Empowering Myself With Today:
_____
_____
_____

Ways I'm Motivating Myself Today:
_____
_____
_____

Ways I'm Bringing Joy into My Day Today:
_____
_____
_____

Monday _____

Date _____

Time	
5 AM	
6 AM	
7 AM	
8 AM	
9 AM	
10 AM	
11 AM	
12 PM	
1 PM	
2 PM	
3 PM	
4 PM	
5 PM	
6 PM	
7 PM	
8 PM	
9 PM	

Top 3 Goals I'm Setting for Myself Today:
_____
_____
_____

Words & Affirmations I'm Empowering Myself With Today:
_____
_____
_____

Ways I'm Motivating Myself Today:
_____
_____
_____

Ways I'm Bringing Joy into My Day Today:
_____
_____
_____

Tuesday _____
Date

Time	
5 AM	
6 AM	
7 AM	
8 AM	
9 AM	
10 AM	
11 AM	
12 PM	
1 PM	
2 PM	
3 PM	
4 PM	
5 PM	
6 PM	
7 PM	
8 PM	
9 PM	

Top 3 Goals I'm Setting for Myself Today:
_____
_____
_____

Words & Affirmations I'm Empowering Myself With Today:
_____
_____
_____

Ways I'm Motivating Myself Today:
_____
_____
_____

Ways I'm Bringing Joy into My Day Today:
_____
_____
_____

Wednesday _____
Date

Time	
5 AM	
6 AM	
7 AM	
8 AM	
9 AM	
10 AM	
11 AM	
12 PM	
1 PM	
2 PM	
3 PM	
4 PM	
5 PM	
6 PM	
7 PM	
8 PM	
9 PM	

Top 3 Goals I'm Setting for Myself Today:
_____
_____
_____

Words & Affirmations I'm Empowering Myself With Today:
_____
_____
_____

Ways I'm Motivating Myself Today:
_____
_____
_____

Ways I'm Bringing Joy into My Day Today:
_____
_____
_____

Thursday _____
Date

Time	
5 AM	
6 AM	
7 AM	
8 AM	
9 AM	
10 AM	
11 AM	
12 PM	
1 PM	
2 PM	
3 PM	
4 PM	
5 PM	
6 PM	
7 PM	
8 PM	
9 PM	

Top 3 Goals I'm Setting for Myself Today:
_____
_____
_____

Words & Affirmations I'm Empowering Myself With Today:
_____
_____
_____

Ways I'm Motivating Myself Today:
_____
_____
_____

Ways I'm Bringing Joy into My Day Today:
_____
_____
_____

Friday _____
Date

Time	
5 AM	
6 AM	
7 AM	
8 AM	
9 AM	
10 AM	
11 AM	
12 PM	
1 PM	
2 PM	
3 PM	
4 PM	
5 PM	
6 PM	
7 PM	
8 PM	
9 PM	

Top 3 Goals I'm Setting for Myself Today:
_____
_____
_____

Words & Affirmations I'm Empowering Myself With Today:
_____
_____
_____

Ways I'm Motivating Myself Today:
_____
_____
_____

Ways I'm Bringing Joy into My Day Today:
_____
_____
_____

Saturday _____
                              Date

Time
5 AM
6 AM
7 AM
8 AM
9 AM
10 AM
11 AM
12 PM
1 PM
2 PM
3 PM
4 PM
5 PM
6 PM
7 PM
8 PM
9 PM

Top 3 Goals I'm Setting for Myself Today:
_____
_____
_____

Words & Affirmations I'm Empowering Myself With Today:
_____
_____
_____

Ways I'm Motivating Myself Today:
_____
_____
_____

Ways I'm Bringing Joy into My Day Today:
_____
_____
_____

My Week in Review

Accomplishments I'm Most Proud of This Week:
_____
_____
_____

Obstacles & Challenges I Triumphed Over This Week:
_____
_____
_____

Ways I Was Kind To Myself & Others This Week:
_____
_____
_____

What I'm Most Grateful For This Week:
_____
_____
_____

Engage Your Goals!

Week #52

"The best way to succeed is to discover what you love and then find a way to offer it to others in the form of service, working hard, and also allowing the energy of the universe to lead you."
~ Oprah Winfrey

Revelations From The Research:

Ludwig, Srivastava, & Berkman conducted a 20-week exercise behavior study found that planfulness – the degree to which a person engages in goal-related thoughts and behaviors – is positively associated with visits to a recreational center, overall physical activity, and writing up descriptive goals.[52]

3 Ps Weekly Action Agenda

Week of _____
Date

Professional:

Actions   Complete By

Personal:

Actions   Complete By

Passions:

Actions   Complete By

Longer Term Actions or Projects:

Commitment Calendar

Sunday _____

Date

Time	
5 AM	
6 AM	
7 AM	
8 AM	
9 AM	
10 AM	
11 AM	
12 PM	
1 PM	
2 PM	
3 PM	
4 PM	
5 PM	
6 PM	
7 PM	
8 PM	
9 PM	

Top 3 Goals I'm Setting for Myself Today:
_____
_____
_____

Words & Affirmations I'm Empowering Myself With Today:
_____
_____
_____

Ways I'm Motivating Myself Today:
_____
_____
_____

Ways I'm Bringing Joy into My Day Today:
_____
_____
_____

Monday _____

Date

Time	
5 AM	
6 AM	
7 AM	
8 AM	
9 AM	
10 AM	
11 AM	
12 PM	
1 PM	
2 PM	
3 PM	
4 PM	
5 PM	
6 PM	
7 PM	
8 PM	
9 PM	

Top 3 Goals I'm Setting for Myself Today:
_____
_____
_____

Words & Affirmations I'm Empowering Myself With Today:
_____
_____
_____

Ways I'm Motivating Myself Today:
_____
_____
_____

Ways I'm Bringing Joy into My Day Today:
_____
_____
_____

Tuesday _____
                                                  Date

5 AM
6 AM
7 AM
8 AM
9 AM
10 AM
11 AM
12 PM
1 PM
2 PM
3 PM
4 PM
5 PM
6 PM
7 PM
8 PM
9 PM

Top 3 Goals I'm Setting for Myself Today:
_____
_____
_____

Words & Affirmations I'm Empowering Myself With Today:
_____
_____
_____

Ways I'm Motivating Myself Today:
_____
_____
_____

Ways I'm Bringing Joy into My Day Today:
_____
_____
_____

Wednesday _____
                                                  Date

5 AM
6 AM
7 AM
8 AM
9 AM
10 AM
11 AM
12 PM
1 PM
2 PM
3 PM
4 PM
5 PM
6 PM
7 PM
8 PM
9 PM

Top 3 Goals I'm Setting for Myself Today:
_____
_____
_____

Words & Affirmations I'm Empowering Myself With Today:
_____
_____
_____

Ways I'm Motivating Myself Today:
_____
_____
_____

Ways I'm Bringing Joy into My Day Today:
_____
_____
_____

Thursday _____
_____ Date

Time	
5 AM	
6 AM	
7 AM	
8 AM	
9 AM	
10 AM	
11 AM	
12 PM	
1 PM	
2 PM	
3 PM	
4 PM	
5 PM	
6 PM	
7 PM	
8 PM	
9 PM	

Top 3 Goals I'm Setting for Myself Today:
_____
_____
_____

Words & Affirmations I'm Empowering Myself With Today:
_____
_____
_____

Ways I'm Motivating Myself Today:
_____
_____
_____

Ways I'm Bringing Joy into My Day Today:
_____
_____
_____

Friday _____
_____ Date

Time	
5 AM	
6 AM	
7 AM	
8 AM	
9 AM	
10 AM	
11 AM	
12 PM	
1 PM	
2 PM	
3 PM	
4 PM	
5 PM	
6 PM	
7 PM	
8 PM	
9 PM	

Top 3 Goals I'm Setting for Myself Today:
_____
_____
_____

Words & Affirmations I'm Empowering Myself With Today:
_____
_____
_____

Ways I'm Motivating Myself Today:
_____
_____
_____

Ways I'm Bringing Joy into My Day Today:
_____
_____
_____

Saturday _____

Date

Time	
5 AM	
6 AM	
7 AM	
8 AM	
9 AM	
10 AM	
11 AM	
12 PM	
1 PM	
2 PM	
3 PM	
4 PM	
5 PM	
6 PM	
7 PM	
8 PM	
9 PM	

Top 3 Goals I'm Setting for Myself Today:
_____
_____
_____

Words & Affirmations I'm Empowering Myself With Today:
_____
_____

Ways I'm Motivating Myself Today:
_____
_____

Ways I'm Bringing Joy into My Day Today:
_____
_____

My Week in Review

Accomplishments I'm Most Proud of This Week:
_____
_____
_____

Obstacles & Challenges I Triumphed Over This Week:
_____
_____
_____

Ways I Was Kind To Myself & Others This Week:
_____
_____
_____

What I'm Most Grateful For This Week:
_____
_____
_____

Engage Your Goals!

Bonus Week

"By recording your dreams and goals on paper, you set in motion the process of becoming the person you most want to be. Put your future in good hands — your own."
~ Mark Victor Hansen

Revelations From The Research:

Oscarsson, Carlbring, Andersson, & Rozental conducted a study of adults who set New Year's Resolutions and found that at a one-year follow-up, those who set approach-oriented goals (focused on achieving a positive outcome) were significantly more successful than those who set avoidance-oriented goals (focused on avoiding a negative outcome).[53]

3 Ps Weekly Action Agenda

Week of _____
  Date

Professional:

Actions Complete By

Personal:

Actions Complete By

Passions:

Actions Complete By

Longer Term Actions or Projects:

Commitment Calendar

Sunday _____

Date _____

Top 3 Goals I'm Setting for Myself Today:
_____
_____
_____

Words & Affirmations I'm Empowering Myself With Today:
_____
_____
_____

Ways I'm Motivating Myself Today:
_____
_____
_____

Ways I'm Bringing Joy into My Day Today:
_____
_____
_____

- 5 AM
- 6 AM
- 7 AM
- 8 AM
- 9 AM
- 10 AM
- 11 AM
- 12 PM
- 1 PM
- 2 PM
- 3 PM
- 4 PM
- 5 PM
- 6 PM
- 7 PM
- 8 PM
- 9 PM

Monday _____

Date _____

Top 3 Goals I'm Setting for Myself Today:
_____
_____
_____

Words & Affirmations I'm Empowering Myself With Today:
_____
_____
_____

Ways I'm Motivating Myself Today:
_____
_____
_____

Ways I'm Bringing Joy into My Day Today:
_____
_____
_____

- 5 AM
- 6 AM
- 7 AM
- 8 AM
- 9 AM
- 10 AM
- 11 AM
- 12 PM
- 1 PM
- 2 PM
- 3 PM
- 4 PM
- 5 PM
- 6 PM
- 7 PM
- 8 PM
- 9 PM

Tuesday _____
Date

- 5 AM
- 6 AM
- 7 AM
- 8 AM
- 9 AM
- 10 AM
- 11 AM
- 12 PM
- 1 PM
- 2 PM
- 3 PM
- 4 PM
- 5 PM
- 6 PM
- 7 PM
- 8 PM
- 9 PM

Top 3 Goals I'm Setting for Myself Today:
_____
_____
_____

Words & Affirmations I'm Empowering Myself With Today:
_____
_____
_____

Ways I'm Motivating Myself Today:
_____
_____
_____

Ways I'm Bringing Joy into My Day Today:
_____
_____
_____

Wednesday _____
Date

- 5 AM
- 6 AM
- 7 AM
- 8 AM
- 9 AM
- 10 AM
- 11 AM
- 12 PM
- 1 PM
- 2 PM
- 3 PM
- 4 PM
- 5 PM
- 6 PM
- 7 PM
- 8 PM
- 9 PM

Top 3 Goals I'm Setting for Myself Today:
_____
_____
_____

Words & Affirmations I'm Empowering Myself With Today:
_____
_____
_____

Ways I'm Motivating Myself Today:
_____
_____
_____

Ways I'm Bringing Joy into My Day Today:
_____
_____
_____

Thursday _____
Date

5 AM	
6 AM	
7 AM	
8 AM	
9 AM	
10 AM	
11 AM	
12 PM	
1 PM	
2 PM	
3 PM	
4 PM	
5 PM	
6 PM	
7 PM	
8 PM	
9 PM	

Top 3 Goals I'm Setting for Myself Today:
_____
_____
_____

Words & Affirmations I'm Empowering Myself With Today:
_____
_____
_____

Ways I'm Motivating Myself Today:
_____
_____
_____

Ways I'm Bringing Joy into My Day Today:
_____
_____
_____

Friday _____
Date

5 AM	
6 AM	
7 AM	
8 AM	
9 AM	
10 AM	
11 AM	
12 PM	
1 PM	
2 PM	
3 PM	
4 PM	
5 PM	
6 PM	
7 PM	
8 PM	
9 PM	

Top 3 Goals I'm Setting for Myself Today:
_____
_____
_____

Words & Affirmations I'm Empowering Myself With Today:
_____
_____
_____

Ways I'm Motivating Myself Today:
_____
_____
_____

Ways I'm Bringing Joy into My Day Today:
_____
_____
_____

Saturday _____
                                    Date

Time	
5 AM	
6 AM	
7 AM	
8 AM	
9 AM	
10 AM	
11 AM	
12 PM	
1 PM	
2 PM	
3 PM	
4 PM	
5 PM	
6 PM	
7 PM	
8 PM	
9 PM	

Top 3 Goals I'm Setting for Myself Today:
_____
_____
_____

Words & Affirmations I'm Empowering Myself With Today:
_____
_____
_____

Ways I'm Motivating Myself Today:
_____
_____
_____

Ways I'm Bringing Joy into My Day Today:
_____
_____
_____

My Week in Review

Accomplishments I'm Most Proud of This Week:
_____
_____
_____
_____

Obstacles & Challenges I Triumphed Over This Week:
_____
_____
_____
_____

Ways I Was Kind To Myself & Others This Week:
_____
_____
_____
_____

What I'm Most Grateful For This Week:
_____
_____
_____
_____

My Goal Getting & Productivity Year in Review

You've had an amazing year filled with documenting your goals and productivity! *In each area of your life, which accomplishments highlight your year? Flip through the pages of this book and allow yourself to reexperience all your successes.*

Relationships	
Career	
Financial	
Living Environment	
Community Engagement	
Physical Health	
Mental & Emotional Health	
Intellectual Growth	
Recreation & Relaxation	
Spirituality	

ENDNOTES

1 Jerabek, I. & Muoio, D. (2017). New Year, New Approach: What It Takes to Achieve Resolutions. Retrieved from https://www.researchgate.net/publication/321918643_New_Year_New_Approach_What_It_Takes_To_Achieve_Resolutions

2 Wang, C., Shim, S. S., & Wolters, C. A. (2017). Achievement goals, motivational self-talk, and academic engagement among Chinese students. *Asia Pacific Education Review, 18(3)*, 295-307. https://doi.org/10.1007/s12564-017-9495-4

3 Locke, E. A. (1996). Motivation through conscious goal setting. *Applied & Preventive Psychology, 5(2)*, 117-124. https://doi.org/10.1016/S0962-1849(96)80005-9

4 Powers, T.A., Koestner, R. & Zuroff, D.C. (2007). Self–criticism, goal motivation, and goal progress. *Journal of Social & Clinical Psychology, 26(7)*, 826-840. https://doi.org/10.1521/jscp.2007.26.7.826

5 Shahar, G., Kanitzki, E., Shulman, S., & Blatt, S. J. (2006). Personality, motivation and the construction of goals during the transition to adulthood. *Personality & Individual Differences, 40(1)*, 53-63. https://doi.org/10.1016/j.paid.2005.06.016

6 Sung, H. K. (2014). Evidence-Based (Simple but Effective) Advice for College Students: Microaction and Macrochange. *The Mentor: An Academic Advising Journal, 16*. https://doi.org/10.26209/mj1661262

7 Brown, T. & Latham, G.P. (2000). The effects of goal setting and self-instruction training on the performance of unionized employees. *Relations Industrielles/Industrial Relations, 55(1)*, 80-95. https://doi.org/10.7202/051292ar

8 Kannangara, C. S., Allen, R. E., Waugh, G., Nahar, N., Khan, S., Rogerson, S., & Carson, J. (2018). All that glitters is not grit: Three studies of grit in university students. *Frontiers in Psychology, 9*, 1539. https://doi.org/10.3389/fpsyg.2018.01539

9 Bjørnebekk, G., Gjesme, T. & Ulriksen, R. (2011). Achievement motives and emotional processes in children during problem-solving: Two experimental studies of their relation to performance in different achievement goal conditions. *Motivation & Emotion, 35*, 351–367. https://doi.org/10.1007/s11031-011-9224-y

10 Claessens, B. J. C., Van Eerde, W., Rutte, C. G., & Roe, R. A. (2004). Planning behavior and perceived control of time at work. *Journal of Organizational Behavior, 25*, 937–950. https://doi.org/10.1002/job.292

11 Evans. L. & Hardy, L. (2002). Injury rehabilitation: A goal-setting intervention study. *Research Quarterly for Exercise and Sport, 73(3)*, 310-319. https://doi.org/10.1080/02701367.2002.10609025

12 Matthews, G. (2015). Goal Research Summary. Paper presented at the 9th Annual International Conference of the Psychology Research Unit of Athens Institute for Education and Research (ATINER), Athens, Greece.

13 Adams, G. A., & Jex, S. M. (1999). Relationships between time management, control, work-family conflict, and strain. *Journal of Occupational Health Psychology, 4*, 72–77. https://doi.org/10.1037/1076-8998.4.1.72

14 Arvey, R. D., Dewhirst, H. D., & Boling, J. C. (1976). Relationships between goal clarity, participation in goal setting, and personality characteristics on job satisfaction in a scientific organization. *Journal of Applied Psychology, 61(1)*, 103–105. https://doi.org/10.1037/0021-9010.61.1.103

15 Morisano, D., Hirsh, J. B., Peterson, J. B., Pihl, R. O., & Shore, B. M. (2010). Setting, elaborating, and reflecting on personal goals improves academic performance. *Journal of Applied Psychology, 95(2)*, 255–264. https://doi.org/10.1037/a0018478

16 Heintzelman, S.J. & King L.A. (2019). Routines and meaning in life. *Personality and Social Psychology Bulletin, 45(5)*, 688-699. https://doi.org/10.1177/0146167218795133

17 Locke, E. A., Shaw, K. N., Saari, L. M., & Latham, G. P. (1981). Goal setting and task performance: 1969–1980. *Psychological Bulletin, 90(1)*, 125–152. https://doi.org/10.1037/0033-2909.90.1.125

18 Wu, S., Matthews, L. & Dagher, G.K. (2007). Need for achievement, business goals, and entrepreneurial persistence, *Management Research News, 30(12)*, 928-941. https://doi.org/10.1108/01409170710833358

19 Wang, W.C., Kao, C.H., Huan, T.C., & Wu, C.C. (2011). Free time management contributes to better quality of life: A study of undergraduate students in Taiwan. *Journal of Happiness Studies: An Interdisciplinary Forum on Subjective Well-Being, 12(4)*, 561–573. https://doi.org/10.1007/s10902-010-9217-7

20 Annesi, J. (2002). Goal-setting protocol in adherence to exercise by Italian adults. *Perceptual and Motor Skills, 94(2)*, 453–458. https://doi.org/10.2466/PMS.94.2.453-458

21 McMillan, D. (2019). What are the effects of goal-setting on motivation and academic achievement in a fourth grade classroom? Retrieved from Sophia, the St. Catherine University repository website: https://sophia.stkate.edu/maed/337

22 Barrett, K. V., Savage, P. D., & Ades, P. A. (2020). Effects of behavioral weight loss and weight loss goal setting in cardiac rehabilitation. *Journal of Cardiopulmonary Rehabilitation and Prevention, 40*(6), 383–387. https://doi.org/10.1097/HCR.0000000000000510

23 Becker, L. J. (1978). Joint effect of feedback and goal setting on performance: A field study of residential energy conservation. *Journal of Applied Psychology, 63(4)*, 428–433. https://doi.org/10.1037/0021-9010.63.4.428

24 Epton, T., Currie, S., & Armitage, C. J. (2017). Unique effects of setting goals on behavior change: Systematic review and meta-analysis. *Journal of Consulting and Clinical Psychology, 85(12)*, 1182–1198. https://doi.org/10.1037/ccp0000260

25 Rubinstein, J. S., Meyer, D. E., & Evans, J. E. (2001). Executive control of cognitive processes in task switching. *Journal of Experimental Psychology: Human Perception and Performance, 27(4)*, 763–797. https://doi.org/10.1037/0096-1523.27.4.763

26 Yukl, G. A., & Latham, G. P. (1978). Interrelationships among employee participation, individual differences, goal difficulty, goal acceptance, goal instrumentality, and performance. *Personnel Psychology, 31(2)*, 305–323. https://doi.org/10.1111/j.1744-6570.1978.tb00449.x

27 Travers, C., Morisano, D., & Locke, E.A. (2015). Self-reflection, growth goals, and academic outcomes: A qualitative study. *The British Journal of Educational Psychology, 85(2)*, 224-41. https://doi.org/10.1111/bjep.12059

28 Ariga, A., & Lleras, A. (2011). Brief and rare mental "breaks" keep you focused: deactivation and reactivation of task goals preempt vigilance decrements. *Cognition, 118*(3), 439–443. https://doi.org/10.1016/j.cognition.2010.12.007

29 Moeller, A.J., Theiler, J.M., & Wu, C. (2012). Goal setting and student achievement: A longitudinal study. *Modern Language Journal, 96 (2)*, 153-169. https://doi.org/10.1111/j.1540-4781.2011.01231.x

30 Schippers, M.C., Morisano, D., Locke, E.A., Scheepers, A.W., Latham, G., & Jong, E.D. (2020). Writing about personal goals and plans regardless of goal type boosts academic performance. *Contemporary Educational Psychology, 60*, e101823. https://doi.org/10.1016/j.cedpsych.2019.101823

31 Aeon, B., Faber, A., & Panaccio A. (2021). Does time management work? A meta-analysis. *PLOS ONE, 16(1)*, e0245066. https://doi.org/10.1371/journal.pone.0245066

32 van der Hoek, M., Groeneveld, S., & Kuipers, B. (2018). Goal Setting in Teams: Goal Clarity and Team Performance in the Public Sector. *Review of Public Personnel Administration*, 38(4), 472–493. https://doi.org/10.1177/0734371X16682815

33 Shivetts, M.S. (2006). Effects of an Individual Goal-Setting Intervention on Goal Orientation, Self-Confidence, and Riving Accuracy in Average Golfers: A Quantitative Design. *Electronic Theses and Dissertations*, 99. https://digitalcommons.georgiasouthern.edu/etd/99

34 Häfner, A., Stock, A., & Oberst, V. (2015). Decreasing students' stress through time management training: An intervention study. *European Journal of Psychology of Education*, 30(1), 81-94. https://doi.org/10.1007/s10212-014-0229-2

35 Teo, T.C. & Low, K.C.P. (2016). The impact of goal setting on employee effectiveness to improve organisation effectiveness: Empirical study of a high-tech company in Singapore. *Journal of Business & Economic Policy*, 3(1), 1-16. https://ssrn.com/abstract=3088132

36 Asmus, S., Karl, F., Mohnen, A., & Reinhart, G. (2015). The impact of goal-setting on worker performance - Empirical evidence from a real-effort production experiment. In *Procedia CIRP* (Vol. 26, pp. 127–132). Elsevier B.V. https://doi.org/10.1016/j.procir.2015.02.086

37 Claessens, B.J.C., van Eerde, W., Rutte, C.G. & Roe, R.A. (2007). A review of the time management literature. *Personnel Review*, 36(2), 255-276. https://doi.org/10.1108/00483480710726136

38 Kokkoris, M. D., & Stavrova, O. (2021). Staying on track in turbulent times: Trait self-control and goal pursuit during self-quarantine. *Personality and Individual Differences*, 170. https://doi.org/10.1016/j.paid.2020.110454

39 Van Yperen, N. W., Blaga, M., & Postmes, T. (2014). A meta-analysis of self-reported achievement goals and nonself-report performance across three achievement domains (work, sports, and education). *PloS one*, 9(4), e93594. https://doi.org/10.1371/journal.pone.0093594

40 Hafner, A., Oberst, V., & Stock, A. (2014). Avoiding procrastination through time management: An experimental intervention study. *Educational Studies*, 40, 352–360. https://doi.org/10.1080/03055698.2014.899487

41 Nelis, S. M., Thom, J. M., Jones, I. R., Hindle, J. V., & Clare, L. (2018). Goal-setting to Promote a Healthier Lifestyle in Later Life: Qualitative Evaluation of the AgeWell Trial. *Clinical Gerontologist*, 41(4), 335–345. https://doi.org/10.1080/07317115.2017.1416509

42 Blankert, T., & Hamstra, M. R. (2017). Imagining success: Multiple achievement goals and the effectiveness of imagery. *Basic and Applied Social Psychology*, 39(1), 60–67. https://doi.org/10.1080/01973533.2016.1255947

43 Van Eerde, W. (2003). Procrastination at work and time management training. *Journal of Psychology*, 137, 421–434. https://doi.org/10.1080/00223980309600625

44 Dominick, J.K. & Cole, S. (2020). Goals as identities: Boosting perceptions of healthy-eater identity for easier goal pursuit. *Motivation & Emotion*, 44, 410–426. https://doi.org/10.1007/s11031-020-09824-8

45 Ogawa, T., Omon, K., Yuda, T., Ishigaki, T., Imai, R., Ohmatsu, S., & Morioka, S. (2016). Short-term effects of goal-setting focusing on the life goal concept on subjective well-being and treatment engagement in subacute inpatients: a quasi-randomized controlled trial. *Clinical Rehabilitation*, 30(9), 909–920. https://doi.org/10.1177/0269215515622671

46 Oliver, J., & MacLeod, A. (2018). Working adults' well-being: An online self-help goal-based intervention. *Journal of Occupational and Organizational Psychology*, 91(3), 665–680. https://doi.org/10.1111/joop.12212

47 Zampetakis, L. A., Bouranta, N., & Moustakis, V. S. (2010). On the relationship between individual creativity and time management. *Thinking Skills & Creativity*, 5, 23–32. https://doi.org/10.1016/j.tsc.2009.12.001

48 Koole, S. L., Smeets, K., van Knippenberg, A., & Dijksterhuis, A. (1999). The cessation of rumination through self-affirmation. *Journal of Personality and Social Psychology, 77*(1), 111–125. https://doi.org/10.1037/0022-3514.77.1.111

49 Masicampo, E. J., & Baumeister, R. F. (2011). Consider it done! Plan making can eliminate the cognitive effects of unfulfilled goals. *Journal of Personality and Social Psychology, 101*(4), 667–683. https://doi.org/10.1037/a0024192

50 Kannangara, C. S., Allen, R. E., Waugh, G., Nahar, N., Khan, S., Rogerson, S., & Carson, J. (2018). All that glitters is not grit: Three studies of grit in university students. *Frontiers in Psychology, 9*, 1539. https://doi.org/10.3389/fpsyg.2018.01539

51 Adhikari, P. & Gollub, E. (2020). O21 initial evaluation of Louisiana's "Small Changes/Healthy Habits" pilot program. *Journal of Nutrition Education and Behavior, 52*(7). https://doi.org/10.1016/j.jneb.2020.04.033

52 Ludwig, R. M., Srivastava, S., & Berkman, E. T. (2019). Predicting Exercise With a Personality Facet: Planfulness and Goal Achievement. *Psychological Science, 30*(10), 1510–1521. https://doi.org/10.1177/0956797619868812

53 Oscarsson, M., Carlbring, P., Andersson, G., & Rozental, A. (2020.) A large-scale experiment on New Year's resolutions: Approach-oriented goals are more successful than avoidance-oriented goals. *PLoS ONE 15*(12), e0234097. https://doi.org/10.1371/journal.pone.0234097

About the Author

With over 20 years of expertise helping people transform their lives and careers, Dr. Colleen Georges is a life and career coach, TEDx speaker, founder of RESCRIPT Your Story LLC, and author of the 8-time award winning book, *RESCRIPT the Story You're Telling Yourself: The Eight Practices to Quiet Your Inner Antagonist, Amplify Your Inner Advocate, & Author a Limitless Life*.

Dr. Colleen's own experiences dealing with and overcoming anxiety, procrastination, perfectionism, and panic attacks have shaped her work helping others. In her TEDx Talk, *Re-Scripting the Stories We Tell Ourselves*, Dr. Colleen illustrates how we can achieve our goals and change our lives by RESCRIPTing the way we talk to and about ourselves. Through RESCRIPT Your Story LLC, she provides individual life and career coaching, leads community wellness groups, and delivers organizational trainings and speaking engagements. Dr. Colleen is also a Rutgers University Lecturer in counseling, women's leadership, and social justice.

She received her Bachelor's Degree in Psychology, Master's Degree in Counseling Psychology, and Doctorate in Counseling Psychology from Rutgers University. Dr. Colleen is a NJ Licensed Professional Counselor, Certified Life & Career Coach, Certified Positive Psychology Coach, Certified Goal Success Coach, Certified Anxiety Specialist, and holds over a dozen certifications in coaching and counseling.

Dr. Colleen's expertise has been featured in various media including News12, RVNTV, Huffington Post, Thrive Global, Forbes, Live Happy, Mashable, The Job Network, Care.com, Aspire Magazine, Formidable Woman Magazine, and New Jersey Family Magazine. She lives in Piscataway, NJ with her husband, José, son, Joshua, and cat daughter, Kitty.

To connect with Dr. Colleen, visit: www.ColleenGeorges.com

RESCRIPT Daily Gratitude Journal

The **RESCRIPT Daily Gratitude Journal** includes 365+ days for you to savor what you are grateful for. It offers resources to help us see there are reasons to feel grateful occurring all the time, but sometimes we must shift focus to notice them, especially during tough times. In the *RESCRIPT Daily Gratitude Journal*, you'll discover: research revelations that illustrate the kinds of thoughts and actions that foster a grateful mindset; that there's always at least one experience, person, accomplishment, or resource to be grateful for; how expressing gratitude can foster increased joy, hope, and optimism; how making time daily to consider what you're grateful for can lead to decreased stress and worry; and strategies for creating daily gratitude practices that support your overall wellbeing.

LET YOUR JOURNEY TO RESCRIPT & THINK THANKFULLY BEGIN!

www.RESCRIPTWorkbooks.com

RESCRIPT THE STORY YOU'RE TELLING YOURSELF:
THE EIGHT PRACTICES TO QUIET YOUR INNER ANTAGONIST, AMPLIFY YOUR INNER ADVOCATE, & AUTHOR A LIMITLESS LIFE

In the 8-time award-winning **RESCRIPT the Story You're Telling Yourself: The Eight Practices to Quiet Your Inner Antagonist, Amplify Your Inner Advocate, & Author a Limitless Life**, Dr. Colleen guides you on a self-authorship journey using the eight practices of her RESCRIPT framework, based in Positive Psychology. You'll discover how to identify limiting stories you're telling yourself that are keeping you stuck; quiet your Inner Antagonist quickly so it doesn't hinder you; amplify your Inner Advocate to cultivate positive thoughts and actions; stop criticizing yourself, dwelling on the past, and fearing the future; and recognize your self-worth so you can set and achieve your goals.

STOP THE NASTY CRITIC INSIDE YOUR HEAD FROM CONTROLLING & LIMITING YOUR LIFE

LET YOUR JOURNEY TO RESCRIPT BEGIN!

www.RESCRIPTBook.com

THANK YOU

My deepest gratitude to my family, friends, clients, students, and readers for always empowering and inspiring me to pursue my goals and passions. This planner could not have been created without you.

With Love,
Dr. Colleen

www.ingramcontent.com/pod-product-compliance
Lightning Source LLC
Chambersburg PA
CBHW081104080526
44587CB00021B/3443